Other Books by Jim Conway and Sally Conway

WOMEN IN MID-LIFE CRISIS
MAXIMIZE YOUR MID-LIFE
YOUR MARRIAGE CAN SURVIVE MID-LIFE CRISIS
TRUSTING GOD IN A FAMILY CRISIS (coauthored with Becki Conway Sanders)
TRAITS OF A LASTING MARRIAGE
WHEN A MATE WANTS OUT

Books by Jim Conway

MEN IN MID-LIFE CRISIS
MAKING REAL FRIENDS IN A PHONY WORLD
ADULT CHILDREN OF LEGAL OR EMOTIONAL DIVORCE

Books by Sally Conway
YOUR HUSBAND'S MID-LIFE CRISIS
MENOPAUSE

Sexual Harassment No More

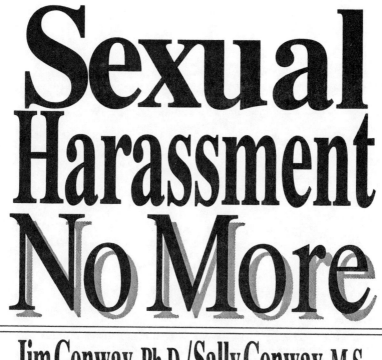

Jim Conway, Ph.D./Sally Conway, M.S.

INTERVARSITY PRESS
DOWNERS GROVE, ILLINOIS 60515

InterVarsity Press® is the book-publishing division of InterVarsity Christian Fellowship®, a student movement active on campus at hundreds of universities, colleges and schools of nursing in the United States of America, and a member movement of the International Fellowship of Evangelical Students. For information about local and regional activities, write Public Relations Dept., InterVarsity Christian Fellowship, 6400 Schroeder Rd., P.O. Box 7895, Madison, WI 53707-7895.

ISBN 0-8308-1631-3

Printed in the United States of America ∞

Library of Congress Cataloging-in-Publication Data

Conway, Jim.
   Sexual harassment no more/Jim Conway, Sally Conway.
      p.   cm.
   Includes bibliographical references.
   ISBN 0-8308-1631-3
   1. Sexual harassment of women.   2. Sexual harassment.   I. Conway,
Sally.   II. Title.
   HQ1237.C66   1993
   305.42—dc20

93-30246
CIP

17   16   15   14   13   12   11   10   9   8   7   6   5   4   3   2   1
07   06   05   04   03   02   01   00   99   98   97   96   95   94   93

To

Michael Schneider
Marc Russell
Craig Sanders
our sons-in-law
who have treated our three daughters and grandchildren
with outstanding
love,
respect,
dignity,
and who are affirming each person in their families so
each becomes the effective person God has planned

PART ONE

Harassment:
A Social
Disease

1
It's Real
& It's Pervasive

W hat's wrong? I'm simply getting what's mine to get. I'm a successful administrator, always have been. And as for my personal life, I'm just like any other red-blooded guy." Nick* would defend himself without embarrassment if asked about his sexual harassment practices over the years.

Nick had earned his master's in social work at a large California university. After graduation he went to work for a state foster care program based in Los Angeles. By his middle thirties he was invited to start a similar program from scratch in another area.

He was to hire all the personnel, including caseworkers, middle-level management and clerical staff. In short, he was given the mandate to set up an office with twenty to twenty-five full-time employees.

Even though Nick was a married man, his hiring practices

In this story and throughout the book we are using real people to illustrate real life. In many cases, however, we have changed names and disguised circumstances to protect the privacy of the people involved.

and the tone he set in the office—over which he had total control—characterize the blatant, unchecked sexual harassment common in the work force and other settings today.

Those Special Qualities

His first employees were secretaries, receptionists and caseworkers. As he hired each woman, he clearly explained he wanted a close working atmosphere where people were friendly with each other on and off the job. Without exception, everyone he hired was in her late twenties, single and blond. None of them was overweight and all were full-breasted. It was as if Nick were stocking his private harem with women who met his special sexual qualifications. They were also dependent upon him for promotions.

The office climate created by Nick was filled with frequent sexual innuendoes, dirty stories, discussions of porno or X-rated movies, and a great deal of touching, hugging and staring. Sometimes the women expressed their uneasiness with the office atmosphere when they talked with each other, but they didn't do anything to change it.

If a woman came into Nick's office to talk about a project or a problem, he would invite her to sit on the corner of his desk. He never looked the woman in the face as he listened. Instead, his eyes would move up and down her body and he would frequently interject a comment such as "You really are an attractive addition to this office."

Then he would add, "I certainly do want you to succeed. I'd like to do all I can to help you so your quarterly performance reviews will show what a valuable person you are. I'm required to send those to the state, you know."

He would frequently follow up his power statement with an invitation for a get-together at a cozy little restaurant where just a few of the office staff would be having dinner. Of course, all except Nick would be women.

A Contagious Sickness

Little by little, Nick kept increasing his control over these women. If a woman was unresponsive, she got a lackluster or negative review with no advancement in pay or rank. She was clearly on her way out. Several quit because they knew they would never get a good review.

Strangely, a sick kind of competition started among the women. Since Nick had made it clear that he needed to promote some of the caseworkers and clerical staff into middle management, they began craftily competing with each other as they tried to win his approval.

Nick systematically invited each woman to spend a weekend with him. He would say privately, "I can promote anybody I want because all of you are very qualified and could easily get the positions I'm looking for." They all knew the *special positions* he was looking for.

He would clearly spell it out. "I'd like you to go with me to a conference on foster care that's being held down in L.A. I want to promote people that I feel really close to. So let's see how close we can get this weekend."

If it weren't for the competitive sickness in the office, someone might have blown the whistle. But these were young women eager to move up and thinking, "What difference does it make if I sleep with the boss a little?" It was common knowledge that they were all part of his harem.

Nick continued to hire and promote only women in their late twenties who fit his sexual standards. The salaries of the promoted women went up fifty percent. However, even though Nick used his power to keep women responding sexually, some of them privately began to resist the pats, hugs and sitting on his desk.

Finally, two women filed sexual harassment complaints with Nick's newly appointed associate director. The associate director, who was herself part of the sexual sickness, assured the women that Nick meant nothing by it: "Let's not spoil our working environment by filing these kinds of complaints. No one else has been bothered—maybe you're just overreacting."

Finally, Daylight in an Ugly World
In Nick's fourth year, the whole Clarence Thomas/Anita Hill debate exploded in the country. It was a big topic of conversation in Nick's office.

Christine, a newly hired woman, quickly assessed the scene. She was soon included in the sexual harassment, but she understood proper sexual boundaries and would not join the sick office system. Within a few months Christine had filed a complaint with the associate director and had talked with the two employees who had filed the previous complaint. Together they planned to go outside the office to get Nick removed. About the same time, surprisingly, Nick started sending out résumés; within a few months he was gone. He assured his staff that they had been great to work with and he was sorry to leave, but it was time for a change.

Christine is a good model for women faced with sexual harassment in the work force. In spite of the associate director's minimizing the situation and unwillingness to act, Christine pressed on. Nick was forced out because she and the other two women were properly assertive.

A woman can expect to meet resistance when she tries to deal with sexual harassment, but times are changing and the law is on her side. Typically, many friends, supervisors, professionals and others in leadership will try to minimize the events. "It really isn't as bad as you think." Another common reaction to accusations of sexual harassment is that of collusion. People who should be expected to help the situation talk behind the woman's back, isolate her from office information and ignore advancement opportunities for her. She may become the scapegoat for all the office problems. "Well, we never had personal conflicts until these sexual harassment charges were filed."

Christine's determination that sexual harassment was wrong and her courage to act to correct it changed the environment of her office. She was not deterred from pressing charges, even in the face of the associate director's rationalization and denial.

Unfortunately, the sexual harassment charges regarding Nick were never acted on, since the harasser was gone. A new director came who was aware of the former situation, and he deliberately created a positive working environment. But Nick took another job. Guess where? A shelter for abused young women, ages fourteen to eighteen. He was employed as the director to organize and staff the new shelter. It would be his responsibility to hire all personnel.

Of course, the coworkers had to be women in a woman's shelter. His special duty was to hire the right women to help these young girls. Guess what these women staffers looked like? Late twenties, single, blond and sexually attractive to Nick. Since it was a residential shelter, Nick—who by now was divorced—would need to live on the premises in order to keep a close tab on things.

Nick is currently working in this shelter, and we suppose that he is continuing to harass young women in their late twenties who fit his sexual fantasies and who can be manipulated to be part of his harem.

The Many Faces of Sexual Harassment
Sexual harassment occurs in many workplaces, but it is not confined to work. Harassing behaviors are also frequently found in the dating scene, marriage, medicine, the military, educational institutions and religious groups.

The word *Tailhook* has come to mean blatant sexual harassment. The nation was shocked and women were outraged as the details started to unfold about what takes place at an annual party in Las Vegas, when active and retired Navy and Marine flyers get together for three days and nights of drunken revelry. Navy Lieutenant Paula Coughlin, a helicopter pilot, launched the investigation into Tailhook '91. In the process, many officers were implicated. Her own boss, Rear Admiral Jack Snyder, was relieved of his command for not responding correctly to her complaints. When Lt. Coughlin reported that she was sexually pawed by her fellow pilots as they propelled her down a hallway in a Las Vegas hotel, Snyder allegedly remarked, "That's what you get when you go on the third floor of a hotel with a bunch of drunken aviators."[1]

The investigation by the Navy was so poorly handled that Navy Secretary H. Lawrence Garrett III was forced to resign after President Bush expressed his displeasure. It grew to involve eighty-three military and civilian women who had been violated by Naval aviators at the convention. The Senate also held up 4,500 Navy promotions and a House committee cut 10,000 jobs from Navy headquarters.

For the next several months, the Navy will consider new evidence against 175 officers, including thirty-three Navy admirals and two Marine Corps generals. Punishment will range from reprimands, reductions in rank and pay cuts to discharge and court martial.

Tragically, Tailhook '91 was considered tame compared to earlier conventions.[2] Perhaps the disgraceful situation is best summed up by the title of one revealing story from *U.S. News & World Report:* "Many Officers, Not Many Gentlemen."[3]

Sexual harassment is wrong—whether in the Navy, a doctor's office, church, an insurance office or a shipping room. It is an out-and-out breach of moral decency by the offender. It's also a violation of the victim's personal boundaries. The end result is a demeaning and shaming of the victim, even if the comments and actions are disguised as flattery.

Not only does sexual harassment damage the victim, but it is also a blight on society. And from our point of view as Christian counselors, sexual harassment is totally alien to the model which Jesus Christ gives us for relating to people.

A Historic Confrontation

In the fall of 1991, Judge Clarence Thomas sat before the United States Senate Judiciary Committee, world television and the American people, facing sexual harassment charges leveled against him by Anita Hill.

The committee's primary responsibility was to assess Judge Thomas's qualifications to sit on the U.S. Supreme Court. But the hearing soon changed focus with Anita Hill's accusations that Judge Thomas had sexually harassed her on many occasions. Judge Thomas denied all of those accusations.

The burning question before the Senate committee and in the minds of millions of people whose eyes were glued to their television sets was, "Who is lying?" They wondered, "How can two people tell such different stories of the same events?"

These were not just ordinary people. Anita Hill was a law professor at the University of Oklahoma. Judge Clarence Thomas had held a number of major positions in government during his career. Ten years before these confirmation hearings, Thomas and Hill had worked together at the Equal Employment Opportunity Commission (EEOC), where the harassment incidents purportedly took place.

In spite of the serious accusations being leveled against Clarence Thomas, the hearings at some points were almost media circus events. The underlying question was, "Is this man fit to be a Supreme Court justice if, in fact, he is lying and if he sexually harassed Professor Hill?"

The committee never did answer the question, "Did Clarence Thomas sexually harass Anita Hill?" However, the all-male Senate Judiciary Committee did decide to recommend confirmation of Clarence Thomas for the United States Supreme Court.

Confused and Shocked

Not only was the nation divided in its opinion of who was telling the truth and whether Judge Thomas should be confirmed, but also a new sense of the reality and pervasiveness of sexual harassment emerged. Suddenly sexual harassment charges were being filed with the federal EEOC in record numbers—up more than 30 percent in 1992 over 1991.[4]

Women were finding the courage to file complaints. If Anita Hill could take the abuse before the Senate Judiciary Committee and the nation, they too would speak out against the humiliation they had so often tolerated.

Most of the nation's women were shocked by the way Anita Hill was treated before the committee. Irene Natividad of the National Conference on Working Women said, "Whether you believe Hill or not, you saw how she was treated. The entire country saw, in a major way, how disregarded and unimportant women are."[5]

A national debate resulted from the televised Thomas/Hill spectacle. Business and industry, education, medicine, the military, service organizations and governmental bodies at all levels were pushed to face the sexual harassment issue. Repeatedly, the discussions showed how very, very far apart men and women are from understanding each other.

A Man's View

Most men still think of sexual harassment in physical terms, but sexual harassment has now been defined to include verbal dimensions and subtleties such as staring at women, winking, calling women "the girls." By law, an intimidating, hostile or offensive working environment is harassment.

In 1980, the EEOC made it clear that sexual harassment is a violation of section 703 of Title VII of the Civil Rights Act of 1964. Some conditions listed by the EEOC are the following:

□ The victim as well as the harasser may be male or female.

☐ The victim does not have to be of the opposite sex.

☐ The victim does not have to be the person harassed but could be anyone affected by the offensive conduct.

☐ The harasser may be the victim's supervisor or an agent of the employer or a supervisor from another area or a coworker or even a nonemployee.

☐ The sexual harassment may occur without economically injuring or resulting in the discharge of the victim.

☐ The harasser's conduct must be unwelcome to the victim when it occurs.[6]

According to the 1980 guidelines, any unwelcome sexual advance, proposition or other sexually aggressive conduct can be considered sexual harassment whenever any of the following occur :

☐ Submission to harassment is made a condition of employment.

☐ The worker's response to the harassment is used as a basis for decisions affecting employment, such as job training and advancement.

☐ Such conduct has the purpose or effect of unreasonably interfering with work performance by creating an intimidating, hostile or offensive work environment.[7]

Clearly, sexual harassment involves social and psychological aspects as well as the commonly recognized sexual affronts, whether verbal or physical. And yet, *many men just don't seem to get it.*

Parade Magazine did a random sampling of men and women on this matter. About men they wrote, "Some did admit to telling dirty jokes. Not one, however, believed he had sexually harassed women. Many said it was the man's role to be the sexual aggressor and to pursue women by asking them out. They thought sexual harassment meant touching, fondling . . . something physical . . .

"Seventy percent of the women polled who served in the military said they'd been sexually harassed. Fifty percent of the women surveyed who work in congressional offices [said] they had been sexually harassed. Forty percent of the women polled who work at federal agencies said they had been sexually harassed."[8]

A Woman's View

Women experience sexual harassment in hundreds of settings: at the grocery store, in their own homes, at church, walking in the park, as well as at work. Sexual harassment to women is very different than to men: "Women [said] they consider 'sexual harassment' to include vulgar language, suggestive jokes, comments about one's body, and pressure to go on dates—especially by a boss or other superior. . . . Verbal harassment is so widespread, it's like bad weather—hardly a reason not to come to work. Most said they wouldn't quit their jobs over sexual harassment unless it got physical."[9]

While many women are sensitive to harassing situations, they feel powerless to correct them. Often they do or say nothing, or they quit work without stating the real reason for leaving. Other women, however, are not so passive and are glad to now have legal grounds to change harassing conditions.

Results of the Thomas/Hill Debate

Several changes followed the hearings. First, *legal certainty and uncertainty* developed. The law is clearly affirming that sexual harassment is legally wrong and can be tried, and that sizable punitive judgments can be levied against harassers and their employers. However, an uncertainty remains: "What is the exact meaning of an 'intimidating, hostile, or offensive working environment'?"

A second result of the hearings is *terror in business*. An article in *The New Jersey Law Journal,* entitled "Harassment, Havoc For Employers: Latest Ruling Charts New Law On Liability and Proof," points out how vulnerable employers are regarding harassment. The case centered around a female manager who accused her boss at Toys 'R' Us of touching her, making lewd comments about her breasts, lifting the back of her shirt and exposing her bra strap.

After six days of trial, the woman was awarded $5,000 in damages because of being touched, but Toys 'R' Us was not held liable for allowing a hostile working environment. However, in a later appeal, all three judges reviewing the case recommended that it be retried. They said, in effect, "Employers cannot shield themselves from liability by arguing they were unaware of the existence of the hostile working environment."[10]

A third result is *confusion in men.* We definitely don't want to group all men as thinking the same about sexual harassment. A large number of men seem to believe that sexual harassment is a problem, but they don't understand that harassment includes more than touching. This group thinks, "If I don't touch, I won't get into trouble." Their view is too narrow.

Unfortunately, another group of men thinks sexual harassment is playful—that a woman ought to feel flattered by remarks such as "I like to watch you walk away from my desk" or "That's a beautiful angora sweater. Do you mind if I stroke it?" Or a man might say in a committee meeting, "We can't expect 'you girls' to understand this." These men must become aware that this kind of behavior is no longer tolerated as it was in the past.

Most men are in the gray area of uncertainty. They ask, "What is sexual harassment? Am I never to comment about a woman's clothing? If a close woman friend of mine gets news at the office that her mother has just died, do I let her cry on my shoulder—or am I supposed to stand back and not touch her?" Many of these men are fearful that their comments, smiles or general friendliness might be viewed as sexual harassment.

It's time for men to realize that sexual harassment is not just a phrase for a temporary fad. This is not a passing anger in women. And we are seeing only the tip of the iceberg. Men must understand that any unwanted sexual advance or innuendo, or any slur about women in general, is being viewed more and more, by women and in the courts, as sexual harassment.

A fourth impact is that *women are becoming more vocal.* As more women enter the labor force and politics, there are more of them to stand together. Women are demanding their rights to be treated as humans and valued for their work contribution, not just for their physical anatomies.

The uncertainty of men about what constitutes harassment and the increased bravery of women have set up a combative or, at the very least, a distrustful environment in many workplaces.

In the seventies and eighties, the singles bars were the places to go if people wanted to date. With the spread of the AIDS epidemic, people began to shy away from the bars and turn to their places of work to connect with someone of the opposite sex. But the awareness of sexual harassment and the restrictions of many businesses have made it totally "off limits" to even think of dating anyone from work.

So What's New?

Today we are shocked at the number of sexual harassment charges being filed. For generations women have been sexually molested and have not said much about it. People had a subtle feeling that women were created for men's sexual pleasure and exploitation and had no rights of their own.

Six decades ago, Elsie was seventeen years old. She went to work as a maid in the home of a very rich man. As she was making his bed one morning, he came into the room and locked the door. She says, "I was scared. He pushed me down onto the bed. He was rubbing all over me. I didn't know what was going to happen. Then, he pulled my dress up and penetrated me. I was shocked at what was happening, but I didn't know what it was all about. I knew it was something that shouldn't have happened. So I asked him if I could leave. He said, 'Don't you dare tell anyone what's happened.' "

When it was obvious she was pregnant, the man fired her. She then told her father what had happened. "He never believed me. Nobody believed me. I have carried the disgrace all my life."

Sexual harassment is a wide spectrum of actions and attitudes, from a pat or a stare to a rape such as Elsie experienced. We want to explore many of these areas and give clear help about how to deal with the wide variety of behavior called sexual harassment.

The Strategy

In the first part of this book we'll look at sexual harassment in various settings such as the workplace, dating life, marriage and family, education and religion.

Following those chapters, we will focus on insights to help men understand women and rise above sexual harassment. Then we'll address women, helping them verbalize their needs and see how they often sexually provoke and harass men.

In the last chapter we'll explore some values to help men and women treat each other with dignity and respect.

Sexual harassment is real and it is pervasive. We believe victims and victimizers alike need to be alerted and educated. Along with helping you understand the problem, we want to coach you on how to prevent harassment—how to be neither a victim nor a perpetrator. In the next chapter, we'll learn why the abuses of sexual harassment are tolerated in the workplace.

2
Sexual Harassment in the Workplace

O ne by one, their voices brimming with rage and sorrow, dozens of California women came forward before a special legislative hearing Thursday to tell of the sexual harassment they have endured at work, sometimes for decades," a story in the *Los Angeles Times* reported.[1]

They were attorneys, hairdressers, high-tech saleswomen, waitresses, a neurosurgeon and a pipe fitter. They had in common graphic and horrifying stories—from a woman police officer whose colleagues made sexual advances toward her to an electrician whose coworkers dumped water on her as she held live wires.

Hairdresser Berna Flanagan of Richmond, California, crumpled into tears as she detailed years of taunts and physical abuse at the barber shop where she worked. Her breasts were pinched by employees as clients watched. She said, "The harassment was constant."

Ultimately, she lost her job and her husband divorced her.

She sued for damages and was awarded $30,000 a year ago by the state Fair Employment and Housing Commission. But she never collected the money because the state Supreme Court ruled that the commission has no power to collect damages.

"Until this day I do not work; I have no money," she said, breaking into sobs. "This is something that lasts a lifetime. It never goes away."[2]

These woman were giving testimony before the California Legislature's bipartisan women's caucus. The goal of the caucus is not only to heighten awareness but also to pass legislation that will protect women by giving them legal recourse when they are sexually harassed.

Do Men Really Do This?

It is interesting that, a month before this caucus, Governor Pete Wilson vetoed a bill that would have enabled victims of sexual harassment to collect cash damages from their employers. In his veto message, Governor Wilson said that it would *"harm business."*

The *Los Angeles Times* article continued: "The twenty-nine women who testified before the women's caucus said employers had rarely taken their complaints seriously. Complaining was career suicide."

The women reported that the harassment ranged from degrading remarks to physical touching. "In many cases male coworkers displayed their sexual organs and threatened women with the loss of their jobs if they did not consent to sex."

The women reported that they tried many different tactics, such as humor or wearing unappealing clothes, in order to ward off the verbal comments and physical touching by coworkers. But none of these strategies worked.

Some Men Just Don't Get It

Mary Gaddis, the first woman in the 1800-member Pipe Fitters

Union, said her mere presence in that male-dominated field was enough to trigger her mistreatment. "What I did was be there."

During the hearing, the caucus released statistics showing that the California Department of Fair Employment and Housing in 1990 handled 50 percent more sexual harassment complaints than in 1986.

The women were angry. Assemblywoman Jackie Speier (Democrat, South San Francisco) lashed out at men and the legislative establishment by saying, "They (men) just don't get it. They're all going to get it before we are finished!"[3]

Sexual harassment in the workplace is extremely widespread. Men seem to think that a woman secretly enjoys such things as:

☐ flirting

☐ a wink

☐ a comment about her body

☐ an arm around the waist

☐ a touch on her knee

☐ a kiss on the cheek

☐ a bump against her breast in a crowded elevator

☐ a direct invitation to have sex

This kind of attention is not acceptable to a woman unless she really is attracted to the man and has some kind of emotional commitment to him. Simply working in the same office is not an emotional commitment.

Many men, however, don't believe that women are uninterested. They think that women actually like this kind of attention and that it's their job to make women feel good—to flatter them with sexual remarks and touching.

One of this book's editors has pointed out that men are confused because different women give different signals. She writes, "Some women—wrongly conditioned by past experiences, perhaps, and using unhealthy patterns for getting their needs met—use flirtatious or even seductive language and gestures. And these women do respond positively when men 'come on to them.' So, men are understandably confused; the same remark can bring a warm response from one woman and a rebuke or cold shoulder from the next.

"One example from TV: David Letterman recently hosted Mary Tyler Moore on his show. He complimented her on looking terrific; when he mentioned her great legs, she looked very pleased and twisted in her seat to give the camera a good view of them. Her short skirt, her smile and her body language all showed she liked David's comments.

"But some other women would have been very uncomfortable to have the same comments made to them—would have resented the almost wolf-whistle tone of voice. Did Letterman harass, then? Not in Mary Tyler Moore's opinion. But he might have said the same thing to another woman and been accused of harassment. No wonder men are confused, these days!"[4]

Be absolutely clear that none of our comments are to be taken as meaning that sexual harassment is okay just because women vary. Nor are we saying that women are to blame. Sexual harassment is wrong—period.

"Come Away with Me"

A fascinating story told by *Washington Post* staff writer Kim Masters points out what women need to do in potentially harassing situations: express a firm "No!" before the situation gets out of hand.

"Ten years ago," she said, "I covered the Equal Employment Opportunity Commission (EEOC) for a trade publication. For some reason, I experienced more harassment of a sexual nature there than I did covering any other federal institution—the Labor Department, the Internal Revenue Service, even the Congress. Call it a curiosity. Certainly it has no bearing on Clarence Thomas who was not then Chairman of EEOC."

At the time Kim was twenty-six years old and thought some of the sexual harassment she experienced was only "business as usual." She told of a conversation with an EEOC official who said, "I'm going to a conference in San Francisco next week. You should come."

Kim replied, "Oh, I don't think my paper would be interested in that."

"You should come anyway, on your own," he persisted.

"Why?" She asked.

"Don't you get it?" he said impatiently. "I'm *propositioning* you!"

"You're married!" Kim said.

She declined the offer and he was good-natured about it even though she turned him down over and over again.

As Kim has gotten older, she is not thinking of sexual harassment as "business as usual." In fact, she says, "I don't have much sympathy for men who say they 'don't get it.' They may not know what it's like to be a woman, just as one individual doesn't know what it's like to be a member of another race. But society requires us to develop sensitivity to racial issues anyway.

"Telling ethnic jokes is a *bad* idea. The same applies to making explicit sexual comments—bad idea. And pursuing sexual quarry at work, particularly among your subordinates? Very bad idea."[5]

The Bad Boys—Your Local Police

For the last few months Southern California newspapers have been filled with articles about sexual harassment in police departments, with such titles as "Harassment Suit Rocks Newport Police" or "Cops Accused of Sex Harassment."

The articles detailed the harassment by saying, "The women—two of them police officers—directed most of their complaints at Police Captain Anthony Villa, accusing him of touching their breasts, knees or legs, verbally harassing the two officers and helping to engineer retaliation in the form of disciplinary procedures when the women refused his advances."[6]

Police Chief Arb Campbell was also named in the lawsuit and is accused of allowing the harassment to continue after the women reported it.

The women have filed a 3.4 million dollar suit against the city, and both Villa and Campbell have been fired. Laguna Hills attorney Michelle Reinglass said, "It is unusual for four women to file suit against an employer, especially a police department."[7]

Even though sexual discrimination was clearly outlawed by federal statute in 1964 and has been more clearly spelled out by other federal statutes throughout the eighties and nineties, many organizations have not provided the harassment-free workplace required by federal law and by some state laws.

Some agencies such as police departments are viewed as very "macho." It's a man's place. When women moved into these areas they were deeply resented by men. Sometimes harassment became a way to protect the "man's job" by driving women out.

Unfortunately, many companies do not have a harassment policy in place. For example, Laguna Beach Police Chief Neil Purcell, addressing hundreds of California police chiefs in 1983, posed the question, "How many of you have written policies against sexual harassment?" He reported that "maybe two hands went up."

Your Tax Dollars Pay for the Harasser's Touch

Because police departments were not prepared, harassment complaints against the departments rose nationwide. And these complaints won sizable judgments.

In 1991, over three million dollars was paid to two female Long Beach police officers as remuneration for harassment. An interesting side note to the Long Beach situation was that 83 percent of the females in the department said that they had been harassed.

Newport Beach and Long Beach are not the only cities in

Southern California to be confronted with harassment cases. Buena Park lost two harassment cases, which resulted in payment of more than $210,000 to two former female police officers—and, at this writing, suits are pending against the Huntington Beach and Garden Grove police departments.[8]

Taking Action

Since the sexual harassment issue has come into the national spotlight, many businesses, agencies and institutions are drafting company policies defining sexual harassment procedures for grievances and penalties for harassers.

A great deal of pressure is on employers, since more and more employers are being sued for not providing a harassment-free work environment. "In 1991 a total of 6,600 sexual harassment claims, costing billions in legal fees, were filed against employers."[9]

Vivian Ross, director of labor relations for McDonald's, said, "Often sexual harassment is in the eye of the beholder. Employers must have a strongly-worded statement, explaining what type of conduct will not be tolerated."

Currently the law focuses on two types of sexual harassment, *quid pro quo* and hostile environment:

Quid pro quo means "You do something for me and I'll do something for you." Often, however, it means "do this or else" and involves a situation in which employment depends on the employee's giving sexual favors to someone: not cooperating can mean demotion or termination.

"Hostile environment" is harassment where the employee does not suffer an economic loss but has been subjected to conduct that is threatening and intimidating in the workplace.

Vivian Ross also pointed out, "Sexual harassment doesn't necessarily have to occur in the workplace to be job-related. It can also happen at an off-site office function, like a Christmas party or a picnic."[10]

No Frosting, Please

I (Sally) am appalled now when I recall a series of events that happened to me during the summer of 1954. The experiences were low-level harassment. Nonetheless, they were a violation against me, and my reactions today would be much stronger than they were then.

I was a newlywed, fresh from the country, holding down my first job in the "big city." Both Jim and I were working to earn money for Jim's graduate school in the fall.

I was pleased to have a secretarial job with the same company where Jim worked delivering bakery goods. While he was selling jelly doughnuts to the women and kids on his route, I was typing letters and adding numbers in an executive office.

For coffee break, we secretaries were allowed to taste some of the day's delicacies in the lounge. To reach it, we had to walk through part of the huge bakery, including a section where the frosting and decorating took place. It must have been coffee time for the rest of the decorating crew each day at that time, because one man, Chuck, always stood working alone beside the gigantic conveyer of pastries.

Now that I think of it, perhaps it was his way of lying in wait for the secretaries who came down the open hallway past his area. If we were in a group, he would just be overly friendly to everyone, wink at no one in particular and flirt as though he were doing us all a favor.

But if I were walking by myself, Chuck would come as close to me as he dared without getting caught in the machinery. He always had a question or a remark to get my attention. And I— coming from a rural area where we were friendly to everyone— would get duped into listening to him.

Then he would begin to make flirtatious remarks and launch into a dirty joke before I could hurry on. Eventually I learned not to go to coffee break alone, but I imagine Chuck had his share of silent laughs and fed his sick fantasies at my expense when my only motive was to be congenial.

Even though I was disgusted by what happened, it would have been unthinkable to take any punitive action. Today I definitely would not put up with his remarks. I would sharply tell him so and would never again be in his presence alone. If necessary, I would go to my boss about the matter.

It's time to stop this male intrusion, or thousands more women may end up as Goldie did. We'll meet her in the next chapter.

3
Sexual Harassment on Dates

I t was a hot July day and I (Jim) wished I could be at a swimming pool. But I needed two summer school courses to officially graduate from high school, so I was doing what I had to do. As I entered the quiet high school, the coolness inside felt good. My mind was in neutral as I climbed the broad stairway to my class on the third floor. As I rounded the last turn, a gorgeous young woman was sitting on the top step, working on her homework.

I was struck by her beauty. Her face was so perfectly formed. She had flawless skin and shining blond hair that fell gently over her shoulders in curls. She was wearing white shorts and a sleeveless knit top. Her perfectly formed legs were crossed. I had to catch my breath as I wondered what this "movie star" was doing here.

As I neared the top of the steps, she glanced up, smiled and said, "Hi!"

I responded weakly, "Hi, are you taking a course here?" She briefly named the course and turned back to her books. I decided then that I was going to arrange for our paths to cross again.

Each day I found Goldie sitting on the steps, doing her last-minute homework before her class started. Soon we became friends and talked more and more about school, our lives and life in general.

Finally, after several days, I got my courage up to ask her for a date. Her response was, "I'd really like to, Jim, but I'm supposed to be going steady with Vinnie."

"Who's Vinnie?" I asked. I knew something was wrong because she didn't turn me down flat. She just said she was "supposed to be going with Vinnie."

Then came an awful story of Vinnie's harassment. He would physically abuse Goldie and any guy interested in her. He forced her, through intimidation and physical violence, to go out with him. The dates were agonizing experiences of intimidation, forced kissing, petting and sexual intercourse.

"Well, I'm not afraid of Vinnie," I thought. "How tough could he be, anyway?" So Goldie and I started dating—very carefully. We went to other parts of the city where Vinnie would not likely be. Goldie always had an excuse ready in case Vinnie called or came by her house while she was gone.

But after a while Vinnie found out about me, and his response was to beat up Goldie. I couldn't believe what I saw the following day at school. This beauty queen looked like a totally different person. She was wearing slouchy clothes, her hair was bedraggled and her face seemed to have been pulverized by a meat mallet. I knew what had happened.

I said to Goldie, "Look, this doesn't change anything. I still want to date you. Forget Vinnie." So I persuaded her to go out with me the next Saturday. I told her, "You don't have to lie. So what if Vinnie finds out? What can Vinnie do?"

I arrived at Goldie's house just before dark, went to the door and was let in by her mousy parents, who seemed very detached from her. Then Goldie and I went out to the car. I opened the door and Goldie hopped in. As I was going around to my side of the car, five motorcycles rode up with Vinnie on the lead bike. Suddenly my words to Goldie were staring me in the face—*what can Vinnie do?* I was about to find out!

Vinnie was off his motorcycle in a flash, grabbed my shirt just below my neck and threw me up against the hood of the car. The rest of his "mafia killers" gathered around to join in verbal derision and to cheer him on as he pounded me.

Vinnie started the altercation with a few well-placed slaps. Then he delivered stomach punches and verbal threats that I truly believed.

He threw me away from the car, walked around to Goldie's side, pulled open the door and yanked her out. He slapped her three or four times and said, "Get on my bike! You're *my* girl! And don't you ever forget that!"

In a moment, they were gone. It was like a bad dream—this vision of loveliness had walked into my life and now she had been carried away on a motorcycle. To what kind of life, to what abuse, to what tragic limitations and demeaning existence? She could have been a beauty queen—but I feared she was now a harassed slave. I never found out, because I never saw her again.

The Size of the Situation

Sexual harassment on dates takes many different forms, from leering at a woman's body, unwanted touching or indecent remarks to forced petting and rape. Even focusing attention on a woman other than the one you're with on a date is a form of harassment.

Sexual harassment on dates is not a small matter. "Results of large-scale surveys of college women indicate that [up to] 78 percent report having been forced to have sexual contact against their will, usually by a person they know."[1]

Not only are these statistics astounding, but so are the contrasting percentages. "When college men were asked about having forced sexual contact on a woman, only 7 to 25 percent believed they had forced her against her will."[2] Surprisingly, the studies also found that "most men who admit to committing sexual aggression deny that they have raped."[3]

Men Don't Care

The crime of date rape became such a problem at Brown University that "female students covered their rest room walls with names of male students they deemed guilty of date rape. The women said they acted out of dissatisfaction with the university's response to their complaints. They stopped when the administration called a campus forum on sexual assault and harassment and strengthened its policies protecting women."[4]

Some people argue that the statistics are artificially elevated and that things are really getting better. But reality is just the opposite.

College men do not believe that they are actually raping women; they think they are only being males—maybe a little sexually aggressive. Some simply do not care whether a woman wants sex or not. They see women as just a body. For example, researchers reported that 26 percent of college men admitted to having made a forceful attempt at sexual intercourse that caused observable distress in the woman (such as screaming, fighting, crying or pleading)[5]—yet these young men don't think of themselves as harassers!

Another disturbing finding is that when college men were presented with a hypothetical situation in which freedom from legal prosecution was guaranteed, 12 to 30 percent of them admitted that they would sexually assault a woman.[6]

Men must be trained to respect a woman's no. And women need to clearly say "No!"

Definition of Rape

A woman is considered raped if she has experienced "penetration against consent through force, threat of force or when she was incapacitated with alcohol or other drugs."[7] This definition, however, covers only a small area of the issue of total sexual harassment on dates.

For instance, there's Goldie's situation. Yes, she was forced to have intercourse, but that was only part of her total harassment. She was physically injured in many ways and her personal being was totally demeaned and trampled.

Many men believe that if a woman goes out with him, he can expect some kind of sexual payoff. And he starts to press for it through unwanted sexual language, unwanted sexual touching, forced petting and/or forced intercourse.

Misinterpreted Sexual Interest

An investigation at Texas A&M University found that men perceive women to be *most willing* for sex when the woman pays for the date expenses. Men believe women are *moderately willing* for sex when the man pays, and men think that women are *least willing* for sex if each person pays his/her own expenses.[8]

To further understand differences between men and women as they view potential date rape, Professor Charlene Muehlenhard of Texas A&M had male college students watch a video of various women on dates. She reported, "The women tried to make clear that they were not interested in having sex, but the male viewers, when questioned about what they saw, could not say with full assurance that the woman did not want sex.

"Even if we put the women in thick, wool skirts and loafers and had them drink iced tea, buckle their seat belts and say upfront they didn't want sex, the male viewers were not convinced." These results and other studies led Muehlenhard to conclude, "Basically there is nothing a woman can do to totally convince a man that she is not interested in having sex."[9]

We personally don't feel the situation is this hopeless. But certainly both men and women need training to deal with sexual harassment.

Another study was conducted by Frank Saal of Kansas State University, in which he showed a video of a male store manager training a female employee. The video was shown to 163 men and women. "Researchers found that the men watching the tape thought that the trainee was acting far more seductive, sexy and flirtatious, than did the women who viewed the tape. In addition, the men also perceived the trainee as being interested in dating the manager, while the women viewers thought she was simply looking for friendship."[10]

In another study, Saal paired male and female college students in a "getting acquainted" conversation. All the women involved in the conversation said they sent no sexual signals, but the male students were certain they did. Saal concluded that men tend to "oversexualize" what women say and do.[11]

When Is "No" Really "No"?

A large midwestern university study discovered a great amount of confusion in *both* men and women when a woman says no. Students were asked to agree or disagree: "If a woman says 'no' to having sex, she means 'maybe' or even 'yes.' " Almost 37 percent of the men agreed with that statement and, surprisingly, over 21 percent of the women agreed.[12]

Earlier studies found that "39.3 percent [of college women] admitted to having said 'no' when they meant 'yes.' "[13] This "token" resistance in women convinces many men that they are not harassing a woman, but she expects a man to pursue her—even if she is saying no!

Attitudes That Contribute to Date Harassment

Most harassers have accepted a certain *package of beliefs* or myths that support their actions. The decision to use sexual language, forced kissing, petting or going "all the way" if possible, has already been made in the harasser's mind because of the false ideas he holds. Some of these are:

☐ If a woman wants to resist rape, she can.

☐ Men must be in charge; women are devious.

☐ Physical force arouses women sexually.

☐ He needs sex.

☐ He has been led to believe she wants sex; therefore, he is entitled.

Men who hold these attitudes tend to believe that sexually harassing a woman on a date—even raping her—is, after all, what she really wants.[14]

A second major influence on whether dating harassment or rape takes place is *peer support.*

Fraternity men are more likely to engage in coercive sexual activities than independent college men. The fraternity men are supported in their aggression by their fraternity brothers. Fraternity men are also more likely to believe it is acceptable to have many sexual partners. In addition, fraternity men are more likely to believe it is all right to get a woman drunk in order to have sex with her.[15]

A third factor is the connection between *alcohol* and all forms of sexual harassment and aggression. Studies have shown that when both parties are drinking, two things are likely to happen: sexual arousal and sexual aggression.[16]

Sex Willingness and Rape Justification
Several factors affect sexual aggression on dates. *Men overestimate a woman's willingness to participate in physical affection or sex.* When men find their dates acting friendly, they frequently feel they are being led on and so are justified in any aggression they may take. This attitude, as we have seen from the previously quoted studies, is intensified if the woman has initiated the date.

We find it interesting that present-day perceptions have not changed much since 1968 when researchers warned, "In most communities, girls are still marked as too eager or too aggressive if they make the first move (ask for the date)."[17]

Another factor is that *men tend to view the world more sexually* than women do. As a result, men believe women are more ready for physical fondling than they are, and women don't know their dates are as eager to make sexual advances as they are.

So it is highly likely that a man will make aggressive sexual moves on a woman, thinking that she wants that. She, on the other hand, will be surprised at what is happening because she has underestimated his sexual eagerness.[18]

An additional factor in the sex-willingness equation is *a person's attitude toward premarital sex*. It probably is not surprising, and studies do verify, that people who feel premarital sex is acceptable are more likely to experience aggression or to be an aggressor leading toward intercourse.

The Problem of Power

The partner who loves the *most* has the *least* power to change the relationship. The opposite is true also—whoever loves the *least* has the *most* power to change the relationship.

Typically, in a sexually harassing dating relationship, the woman loves the most and is afraid to lose the man she's dating. Her strong love for him and fear of losing him set her up to be a victim of the man's harassment.

On the other hand, the male sexual harasser loves the least and so feels he has little to lose. If he can't get this woman into the sack, lots of other women will be willing. So he doesn't care if he throws this one away. What does he have to lose by being aggressive?

If she says, "I don't ever want to see you again," he hasn't lost much because he hasn't loved much. Therefore, it's easy for the person who loves the least, in this case the male aggressor, to be the sexual harasser in a dating relationship. If the love/ power relationship remains *unequal,* we have a situation like that of Goldie, who probably has been victimized all her life.

If women understand this power issue and become more self-confident about their goals and purposes in life, they will be less likely to be victims of sexual harassment on dates. We will talk more about this later in the book.

Women, Use Your Power!

As the dating process continues so that each partner loves equally, then both gain power and both are able to achieve the long-range goals they want from this relationship—marriage, lifelong commitment, home and family.

A woman must use her power in the relationship to stop her dating partner. He has been socialized to be aggressive. His peer group reinforces aggression. His hormones encourage it. She may be able to use her power of "no, not until we're married" to help transform this aggressive bachelor into a husband who will commit himself to care for a family. Her influence may move him from being a predator to a protector.

But we are not encouraging women to continuing dating a predator in order to reform him. When he becomes aggressive, say "No!" If he reforms himself and respects you, then keep dating. Otherwise protect yourself by not dating this man again.

When Date Rape Occurs

Sexual harassment on dates—especially the criminal act of date rape—leaves tremendous psychological wounds. If a woman doesn't deal with the emotional issues, she will experience greater injury from the psychological damage than from the physical harassment or attack.

If you're a woman like Goldie who has been pushed beyond your sexual limits, consciously or unconsciously you'll feel dirty, ashamed, different from other people and, therefore, lonely. These feelings set up a scenario where you are likely to be victimized again and again.

You should take advantage of workshops for sexual harassment or rape recovery, or free counseling sessions, available at colleges, universities, churches or community mental health centers.

Shame is one issue to be resolved. A frequent reaction to unwanted sexual aggression is the desire to take frequent baths to wash away a "dirty" feeling. Your feeling of shame may be connecting to your guilt mechanism. Maybe you're saying, "If only I hadn't worn that outfit. If I had just stopped him earlier. If I wasn't so afraid to lose him. . . ."

No matter what you did or didn't do, his sexual harassment and aggression are *wrong!* Believing that will help you bring the situation into proper perspective.

Anger is a second issue. Included in the anger issue is your belief that you ought to forgive people. If you bury the anger and quickly "forgive" before you truly understand the situation and deal with the aggressor, you're not going to help the aggressor nor stop his harassment. You are likely to be a repeat victim and repeat "forgiver."

Anger is given to you by God. It can put some stiffening in your backbone, so that you'll finally say, "Enough is enough! Stop! That's it! Buzz off, Charlie!" (Or whatever else you would say.) Don't be afraid of anger. It's your ally to help you resolve your pain.

Ultimately, as anger works its purpose—making the necessary changes in you and the men you date—you'll be able to move freely to the area of forgiveness. By then your forgiveness will not set you up to be a future victim.

Trust is another emotional factor. You've been betrayed! You thought this person loved you and wanted only the best for you. Doesn't he care how you feel? You've lost trust not only in the sexual harasser but also in your own perception. You were dead wrong when you assessed the sexual interest of your harasser. Now you're not going to trust yourself to make a correct estimate of any man. Again, this lack of trust is actually a gift from God. See it as a friend. This lack of trust can help you firm up your boundaries. It will also help you readjust your thinking about the sexual readiness of men and take preventative steps so that you will not be a victim.

If you have been sexually harassed on dates, your trust of men has been affected. You can be assured, though, that someday you'll be able to trust men again. As you begin to date men who are trustworthy, you'll find your trust will return.

At first you had a blind trust which believed that someone who professed love would not exploit you—but he did. Now as you date *trustworthy* men, you will have an *informed* trust and can say, "I know you could sexually exploit me, but I know my boundaries, and I choose to trust you." Establishing stronger boundaries and clarifying your thinking about men will make it easier for both you and your new partner to clearly understand and trust each other.

Loneliness is another issue that must be faced. Typically, the victim of dating harassment wants to run away and hide. She feels as if she is the only woman who has experienced this humiliation, especially if she has not been in recovery groups where people have talked freely of sexual aggression and rape.

Resist the temptation to hide. It's crucial to connect with support groups, counseling help and close female friends who will help you work through the isolation. You ultimately will be able to use your tragic experience to prevent it from happening again to you. You'll also be able to help other women recover.

Reducing the Potential for Harassment on Dates
To change the real-life statistics, we need men to be less sexually

aggressive and women to be more assertive in saying, "No!" Plus, each person needs a more accurate perception of the other's sexual readiness.

Women need to understand and talk about their boundaries. Men need to understand and respect their own boundaries as well as their date's. For example, both of you need to consider the implications of drinking and set strict limits, since alcohol promotes sexual aggression. Both need to set a time deadline. To illustrate, you may decide together that your dates should not last more than six hours. You should mutually agree to prohibitions against certain activities, such as heavy petting or being naked with each other.

Women should not underestimate power in a dating relationship. They need to fully comprehend the connection between loving the most and having the least power. They should focus on life issues that are bigger than their immediate dating partner. In that way, they will have power to transform the dating relationship into a positive experience for both. Or, if that doesn't happen, they will be able to pick up and move on with their life intact.

The Importance of Values

A fascinating study was done at Pennsylvania State University about the impact of Roman Catholicism on forcible rape. The results showed that the greater the number of Catholics in a given population, the lower the number of rapes that occurred, as well as other sexual deviances.[19]

This study also showed that people who were Catholics in name only (they did not accept the Catholic code of sexual conduct) were not as likely to have their behavior modified. Therefore, it is not simply a matter of belonging to or attending church; rather, it is having strong beliefs about the wrongness of sexual harassment and aggression so that a person's behaviors are appropriate.

Later in the book we'll talk more about what men need to know about women and how both men and women need to help each other understand each other. For now, this list of positive attitudes and actions will help focus your present relationship on mutual friendship instead of merely sexual conquest:

☐ Spend more time in public places talking with each other, rather than trying to control your hormones in the back seat of a car or in your apartment.

☐ Serve the other person and let him or her serve you. Try to understand what will help that person become the very best he or she can possibly be.

☐ Relax. If God is in this relationship, you don't need to rush it. The growth of something permanent takes time.

☐ Be courteous and understanding. Harassment is self-serving exploitation. Courtesy and understanding enable each person to accept a no, because there is a respect for the person.

☐ Affirm. Praise each other. Be the very best cheerleaders for each other.

☐ Ask what each other wants in the way of physical touching. Is it a kiss, a hug? Listen carefully and don't assume more than what is spoken.

☐ Encourage spiritual development. A verse in the Old Testament gives interesting insight about the connection between knowing God and success in life. It says simply, "But the people that do know their God shall be strong and do great deeds."[20] Help your friend to know God deeply so that life's accomplishments and joys will be greater than his or her wildest dreams and imaginations.

4

Sexual Harassment in Marriage

Rob and Pam's marriage in the early seventies should have been the beginning of a storybook adventure. Rob and his parents had moved into Pam's town when he was a senior in high school. At first he felt very much adrift in this new setting, but soon he was involved in a full round of sports activities.

Pam was an attractive girl who was also a very popular leader. She dated a lot, but when she met Rob her interest in other guys disappeared. Pam and Rob both felt an instantaneous attraction. They began a steady dating process that culminated in their marriage right after high-school graduation the following June.

During their dating months they had been extremely affectionate. Pam's comment was, "We could hardly keep our hands off each other." In fact, they had crossed over their own commitment lines, and in the heat of passion they had intercourse several times before they were married.

All of this affection was very private, however. After they

were married, Pam wanted the world to know how much she loved Rob. So on several occasions she was publicly very expressive about her affection for Rob.

That was one of their first major battles. Rob didn't want her to be sexually assertive in front of other people, especially his parents and relatives. He felt he was being sexually pursued by his wife. He had loved her aggressiveness before marriage, but now he wanted her only when *he* wanted her.

The Woman's Place
It became obvious after awhile that Rob not only resented public affection but had other strong convictions as well. He began to tell Pam clearly that a woman had "a place" and she needed to stay in her place. That was a shock to Pam and she asked, "What do you mean I'm supposed to stay in my place?"

For the first time, Rob let Pam know his views of marriage and women. To Rob, a woman wasn't to work outside the home. She was to stay home and raise the children. She was to support and encourage his ventures and be available to him if and when he wanted a sexual encounter.

It became clear to Pam that Rob's view of a wife was that she be a sexual servant, child raiser and homemaker. All of their talk of companionship had been "just talk."

Pam actually had a higher sexual need than Rob, and he used that to control her. During her twenties, Pam tried to fit the mold that Rob set up for her, but as she moved into her thirties she felt an urgent desire to be involved in fuller dimensions of life than just staying at home and doing his bidding.

She got involved in activities at their kids' school and their church and began attending self-improvement seminars. Each time, however, Rob criticized her for taking time away from home.

Finally Pam decided to take a part-time job. That really drew Rob's wrath. It was a threat to him as a provider. Reluctantly he let her take the job, but he started nonstop harassment. He demanded sex when Pam was under great pressure. He'd sneeringly say, "You're the one who always wanted sex—well, now I want it." When he forced himself on her sexually, she was reluctant to participate with him, and he would then accuse her of having an affair. As he hacked away and repeatedly humiliated Pam, their marital relationship eroded.

Unfortunately, Rob hadn't done any growing after they were married, so he couldn't understand Pam. The more she grew and reached out for a more rounded expression of God's purposes for her, the more terrified Rob became. In reaction, he belittled, harassed and put down his wife even more.

Sexual Confusion
Sexual harassment in marriage takes many forms. Often it comes from a misunderstanding of the sex act itself by both husband and wife. Unconsciously, each partner thinks his or her mate has the same response to sex as he or she does.

Women often think of sex as a warm, caring, sharing experience that involves the psychological and spiritual, as well as tenderness and a deep commitment. When a wife sees that her husband is interested in sex, she automatically thinks he's viewing sex in the warm, cuddly way she does. He, however, walks into the kitchen, slaps her on the rear, grabs her breasts and says, "Let's go to bed." She is disillusioned and feels that he must not truly love her or he would not come at her this way.

Many men, on the other hand, assume that women have the same instantaneous turn-on mechanism as males. So a husband who has just slapped his wife on the bottom and massaged her breasts can't understand why she doesn't turn around and say, "Boy, I'm really hot for you. Let's go to bed."

The Difference
It would be helpful if couples understood that men are usually

like gas stoves while women are generally like electric stoves. When you turn on a gas burner, it's instantly on. As soon as you turn it off, the flames are gone and the heat disappears. Most men are like that. Only a small stimulus is needed to turn them on. Then, as soon as men ejaculate, they may give a few more hugs and kisses, but, essentially, they're off to sleep. Or they get out of bed, put on their pants and say, "I've gotta go now."

When you turn the burner to high on an electric stove, you can put your hand right on the burner at first. It's still cold; nothing is happening. You look at the switch and ask, "Did I turn it on yet?" You did. By and by, it starts to get warm, then hot. Pretty soon it's red hot.

Then you shut it off. But it's still red hot. You've turned the switch off, but it's still glowing. Gradually it starts to cool down, and after awhile the heat is gone.

Most women are generally like that electric burner—slow to warm and slow to cool. Men, however, are designed to be instantly on and instantly off. The misunderstanding of this sexual difference often leads to mistreatment by one or both partners.

Each person may feel exploited and unloved. A process of belittling, insulting and forcing sex may start—a process which could poison the marriage. Sex becomes an unwanted, demanded duty for the wife, making her feel she is nothing more than a legal prostitute. The husband thinks his wife is frigid and he has been misled and cheated.

Same Scene; Different Responses

To illustrate that women are sexually different from men, in our marriage seminars, we sometimes say, "Suppose a twenty-five-year-old, well-built, naked man ran across the stage right behind us. What would be the reaction of you women?"

Typically, women in the seminar begin to giggle. They have

a good laugh over this guy caught with his pants down. But they're not at all thinking about going to bed with him just because he's naked.

Then, we say, "Now suppose a twenty-five-year-old woman with a great body runs across the stage naked. How would you men react?"

It's interesting to watch the men. Some of them turn beet red. Almost all of their eyes dilate, and we can see the pictures beginning to click through their minds.

To these guys, it's not funny; this is a sexual possibility! They wonder what it would be like to chase her behind the curtains. Many of these guys fantasize that she came onto the stage naked to attract them *alone* to a sexual encounter.

What Turns Her On?

Well, what *does* attract a woman? If a husband doesn't figure it out, he's going to have lots of years of low-level sex. If he decides that it's his wife's fault and he changes partners, he'll have the same trouble, because he's still relating to a woman.

From the woman's point of view, three things are necessary for a good sexual relationship:

☐ the right person
☐ the right time
☐ the right setting

For a woman to have a good, loving sexual experience, she needs not just one but *all three* conditions to be right, or she feels she's being used. Many, many men miss it in all three areas.

The right person is an intelligent man, self-confident but not arrogant, who understands her. The right man is honest with himself and her. He also takes care of his body and his grooming. Men are all hung up on muscle or penis size when women are looking for a quality *person*.

Many men are interested in quickie sex, but for the woman, the time has to be right. If you come home from work and greet your wife after she has had a hard day at work, you might be thinking it would be great to have a little "afternoon delight." You hug her a little bit, start massaging her buns and kiss her on the neck. Then within thirty seconds you say, "Let's go do it." That's the wrong time.

For a woman to have a free, open and pleasurable sexual encounter, she needs a time when she's not rushed by other demands. You may be able to pull her into the bedroom, and because she loves you, she may have sex with you. But let us assure you, you're only having sex with her body. Her mind is wondering about dinner, stuff that happened at her job that she wants to talk to you about, and whether the kids are okay.

Let's continue the illustration of you two meeting in the kitchen after work. You are the right person. (You would be more of the right person if you really understood the anxiety she is wrestling with.) She wants to respond to you, but you don't seem to understand that it's the wrong time. It's not on her agenda to have fast sex—in and out of the bedroom in seven minutes flat.

It's also the wrong *setting*. The kids are watching TV, but they're also periodically roaming around the kitchen, looking for snacks. They're hollering, "What's for supper?" or "Help me with my homework." She fears that at any minute they might come through the bedroom door. She's tense. She can't get turned on in such a setting. She desperately wants to please you and may have sex with you physically—but her spirit and emotions need a secure environment.

Tragically, many men out there respond at this point by saying, "Her body's enough for me. I'll take that." If you do have sex that way, you're gradually eroding your marriage. Repeatedly, you are convincing your wife that you don't really care about her as a person and you'd be willing to jump into bed with any available woman.

What Is Sexual Harassment in Marriage?

Sexual harassment in marriage is probably one of the best-kept secrets. The tragedy is that husbands, wives and even children become conditioned to accept sexual harassment in other areas of life because it is such a common experience in marriage. The harassment events and feelings cover a wide range, from negative comments about the other person's body or sexually inadequate performance to actual marital rape.

Pornography can feed the problem. The women pictured in magazines and films are touched up and paid to perform. If a husband believes that all women are like these pornographic women, he may start a process of harassment, belittling and humiliation that dampen his wife's sexual drive and destroy her self-image.

Perhaps the most common forms of sexual harassment in marriage are withholding sex and demanding sex. These actions are not really about sex but about power. Sex is used as a tool to manipulate the other person to do what you want him or her to do.

Sexual harassment in marriage also has a violent dimension. Many wives are forced to have sex—literally are raped. The kind of husband who commits "legal rape" justifies himself on the basis that he is married to this woman and he has a right.

Frequently physical beatings are attached to the rape, especially if the wife doesn't submit quickly enough or participate actively enough.

Marital Sexual Harassment Spills into Other Areas

The difficulty about the issue of sexual harassment in marriage is that it is so common that people tend to overlook it as truly being sexual harassment. Yet it is probably accurate to conclude that most marriages have experienced some degree of sexual harassment at some time.

Because harassment in marriage is so common and so frequent, it conditions each partner, and ultimately the children, to be harassers or to accept harassment in many other areas of life—work, dating, religious settings, the legal profession, the medical profession, the counselor's office, the military, the supermarket, the school grounds—almost every area where males and females are in frequent and extended contact with each other.

Tragically, sexual harassment in marriage is subtly encouraged by many religious systems. Being a submissive victim is consciously or unconsciously glorified. So then sexual harassment in marriage is reinforced, and also women are more likely to be vulnerable to a religious leader's sexual harassment.

In a coming chapter, we ask, "Why do women accept it?" Then we'll ask, "Why do men do it?" Certainly the frequency of sexual harassment in marriage sets up both males and females to harass and be harassed.

Factors That Increase Sexual Harassment in Marriage

Any baggage that people carry from their parental home, their personal experiences as a child or teenager, or traumas from previous marriages will have a direct bearing on marital sexual harassment.

For example, if people are addicted to alcohol, drugs or pornography, they are more likely to be sexual harassers. Similarly, if people carry some other form of dysfunction from their parents' home, or if they were raped or sexually abused, they will be more likely to think of themselves as victims or to victimize their mate.

The Other Woman/Man Syndrome

Another sexually harassing experience in marriage is when a husband is stimulated by another woman and goes to bed, expecting his wife to care for his sexual arousal. He may have been turned on by a sexy movie, a provocative video or a pretty waitress who kept coming on to him while they ate dinner. Women resent being used as a masturbating device while the husband is sexually fantasizing about another woman.

Harry told his wife repeatedly that she was ignorant, came from a crazy family, didn't have enough education, didn't have any skills or abilities, couldn't do anything right. He let Martha know that the only reason he stayed with her was that he was trapped by a legal marriage document. He felt cornered because the church he belonged to opposed divorce.

He told Martha, "I don't love you. I never have. It was a mistake to have married. It was not God's will; therefore, in God's eyes, I'm not really married. I am free to have relationships with any other women I choose. And it's none of your business."

Harry lived exactly like that. At church, he would hug and fondle any woman he could. He was smiling, friendly, would go out of his way to take a woman home, fix a broken appliance in her house or help her with "spiritual matters."

In a restaurant, Harry would flirt with the waitress and female customers who were seated nearby, even though he was supposedly eating dinner with his wife. Actually, most of the time he arranged for them to eat out with other people so that he didn't have to be alone with his wife. Harry and Martha were married over fifty years. Martha endured this harassment for her entire married life, until the very moment she died.

Some women spend their lives looking over their shoulder, wondering if their husband is involved with another woman. Sometimes you'll see a wife watching her husband's eyes as he looks around a crowded restaurant or room. She's wondering, "Who is he looking at and how do I measure up?" That's a terrible harassment to live with day after day.

Martha didn't even have to look over her shoulder to see if Harry was looking at other women. She knew he was! He made it clear that he would ogle as he pleased.

At one point, we asked Martha why she didn't leave Harry. She responded, "Half a man is better than no man."

She couldn't face living alone and she was certain she would not be a likely candidate for remarriage. So she settled for Harry's continued harassment and humiliation.

Don't fool yourself. Harassment in marriage won't go away until you talk about it. If you don't, you may end up like Martha—harassed, exploited and victimized all your married life.

Modeling the Greatest

The servant attitude of Jesus Christ runs counter to our culture in general and is frequently missing even in the Christian subculture. But Jesus' humble ministering to others—while still remembering who he really was[1]—is the ultimate model for us all. Why is it that males skip over Jesus' servant teachings and demand "bosshood" in their homes? Many men, including theology experts, are blind at this very point. They assume that their wives are not their equals and therefore should fill lesser roles in marriage, the church and society.

Frequently these men are insecure about their lives or their maleness. We like the bumper sticker that reads, MEN OF QUALITY ARE NOT THREATENED BY WOMEN SEEKING EQUALITY. Even more to the point, men of quality will *help* women have equality.

Some men have adapted to our contemporary cultural changes for women, but many still try to run their marriages "the way Dad did."

People sometimes use the concept of "headship" from Ephesians 5 as a basis for male dominance. If headship is interpreted as meaning privilege, authority and dominance, we violate the meaning of that section of Scripture and of Christ's teaching and modeling. Headship more accurately means "source," as in source of life and nourishment. (See the analogy of man with Christ in Ephesians 1:22; 4:15; 5:23 and Colossians 1:18; 2:18-19.)[2]

Unfortunately, in many marriages headship indicates male privilege, which is then interpreted as, "I get to do the things I want to do." "Family decisions are primarily for my benefit." "Money is spent to promote my ambitions." The wife and children are to be contented with whatever is left over.

A Mutual Marriage

We feel an additional note about marriage values is important. Following Christ's example of respecting and serving others will lead a couple to live out a mutual marriage. Some ingredients essential to that kind of relationship are the following:

Mutual Valuing. If I really believe that all are created equal and God has given each of us gifts to be used to strengthen other people, then I must believe that God also has given valuable abilities to my mate.[3] God values my mate as much as he values me. He has entrusted gifts and abilities to him or her, even though they may be different from mine.

The Genesis account of creation points out that Adam was created incomplete. Eve was a counterpart to complete him. Eve was also incomplete and needed Adam. We humans are not born as whole entities. We cannot live as isolated islands in the sea or as hermits in the desert. We are created by God to be in relationship, each contributing to another's life.

Happily married couples appreciate what they each bring to the relationship. Their union is more than just addition. One plus one now multiplies to equal a deep sense of valuing and being valued.

Mutual Responsibility for Growth. We are not just rooming-house boarders, living separate lives. We are people accountable to each other. The growth of my mate is directly correlated to my investment of concern, time and energy in helping him or her grow.

Sometimes one person is up and the other down; one is weak and the other strong. Throughout marriage our strong and weak roles will continue to switch. A mutual marriage assumes that whoever is stronger at the moment will be responsible to encourage and support the one who is temporarily weaker. The partners take turns going the second mile so that both can survive and grow.

Mutual Submission. In a mutual marriage, it is *not* that one is the boss (generally the husband) and the other a servant (often the wife). Instead, two servants offer to each other their gifts and abilities, each honoring, respecting and loving the other.

Jerry and Barbara Cook, the authors of *Choosing to Love,* have aptly defined this servanthood type of submission:

"True submission does not deny my own value or negate our differences. It *offers* my ideas, opinions, and strengths to you with the motive of adding something to you that only I can give; but this is an *offer*, not a command; a sharing, not a takeover; a giving of myself, not a power play.

"In submitting to you I do not give up my true self; rather I give *out of myself*, not denying who I am but offering who I am as an act of love and trust. True submission cannot take place if I deny my true self because I then have nothing of substance to offer to you—not a real person, only an empty shell."[4]

5

Sexual Harassment in Education

Philip was the chairman of the sociology department at a West Coast university. He was an attractive man in his early forties who had a winsome personality and loved to sail. In fact, he owned his own forty-foot sailboat.

Phil was recently divorced. His wife walked out, saying, "I've had it. You're sexually sick and you're just using your position at the university to feed your sickness."

Phil taught at the graduate level. As a result, his classes were small and he spent a lot of personal time with students, working on research projects, helping them get grants and assistantships and overseeing their thesis writing.

Phil was a powerful man, not only in the eyes of his fellow professors but also with the university administration which had made him department chairman. But Phil had an even more powerful position with his students. He could make success happen for them or he could smash their educational dreams forever.

Much of a graduate student's potential achievement depends on the professor's personal commitment to the individual student. Graduating with a Ph.D. is a combination of student grit and political influence within the department. Typically, 75 percent of doctoral students in the country never finish their programs. Students and faculty alike know that it takes a great deal of commitment on the part of the faculty, as well as the student, to complete the degree.

"Sailing School"

Since Phil loved to sail and because many of his classes, seminars and study groups were very small, he would often invite students to go sailing with him as they studied.

These excursions were lively, meaningful times as they sailed up the coast, then dropped anchor and sat around exchanging ideas and enjoying the sun. The students really *did* learn and were helped along toward their eventual doctoral degrees. But the students who went on these trips were always specially selected.

Phil offered a sailing seminar to one of his larger classes but said that it would be limited to six students whom he would choose.

Surprise! The six he chose were the prettiest women with the best bodies. One of them, Jennifer, especially fit all of Phil's "qualifications" for a candidate. She frequently flattered Phil and generally was in awe of him.

Phil was drawn to her affirmation, her willingness to learn as a student and her sympathetic understanding of his divorce. But he was also drawn to her well-built body.

Red Sails in the Sunset

Phil often invited Jennifer alone for sunset cruises up the coast so that they could talk about her studies, internship and research project. They strategized about the steps she needed to take during the next three years to complete her doctoral degree. Typically, they talked as they ate dinner on the boat. Then Jennifer settled into Phil's arms as they watched the sun set and spent the evening making love.

After a couple of years, Jennifer started pressuring Phil for marriage, but he was unwilling to commit to her. Jennifer finally realized that he was just using her, but she was trapped. "Do I put up with his sexual use of me to get a degree? Am I just buying my Ph.D. by being 'bedded'? Will I always wonder if I made it on my abilities or on my breast size and pretty face?"

When Jennifer raised these questions with Phil, he told her that he could only be her advisor if she continued to have sex. Jennifer decided to endure the sexual humiliation in order to get her degree. In her mind it was a choice between enduring another eight months until graduation or completely dropping her Ph.D. hopes.

The Professor's Power

A frightening slogan is practiced all too often in educational circles: "An A for a lay."[1]

The problem in academia is much larger than just getting better grades by going to bed with professors. It's the problem of power! In college and university settings, the professor not only has power over a student's grades, but also over student appointments, comments in the student's permanent record, contacts for future job opportunities or career advancement, and the student's acceptance with other professors in the institution.

College campuses abound with examples of sexual harassment. N. T. Truax, director of the Women's Center at the University of Minnesota, said, "Some professors cause problems because they believe their right to academic freedom is absolute.

"I've sat in meetings where faculty members have said that academic freedom gives them the right to take a woman aside and feel her breasts. To me, that is a warped sense of academic freedom."[2]

A Yale undergraduate charged her political science professor with sexual harassment. She said he offered her an A in exchange for sexual favors. She refused and received a C in the course. She has since filed a lawsuit against the university.

A senior communications major at a California state university testified before the California State Legislature that she knew of "at least 15 professors who offered 'A's' for sex."

A female cadet at West Point left the military academy after charging her male squad leader with improper sexual advances. The academy dismissed her charges when the squad leader denied any wrongdoing.[3]

At University of California—Berkeley, a group of female sociology students organized themselves as Women Organized Against Sexual Harassment (WOASH) and waged a campaign against professors whom they felt were using the 'power of the grade' to elicit sexual favors.[4]

Heads in the Sand

Until recently, however, little has been done to recognize sexual harassment of women students. Many studies have documented the fact that female workers are vulnerable to sexual abuse by male employees,[5] but less attention has been given to the problem in educational circles.

Until the middle seventies, there wasn't a definition for this fuzzy area—these uncertain events and feelings that something wrong was happening. Everyone could clearly define rape, but they didn't know what to call the sexual aggression that didn't end in rape but left women feeling very uneasy about themselves and the sexually offensive men.

The term apparently was first defined in May 1975 in a survey developed by the Women's Section of the Human Affairs Program at Cornell University.[6] Once these unwanted sexual advances finally had a name—"sexual harassment"—there followed an attempt by many schools and organizations to refine a specific definition: "What is sexual harassment?" Working Women United Institute has defined sexual harassment as "verbal sexual suggestions or jokes; constant leering or ogling; 'accidental' brushing against your body; a 'friendly' pat, squeeze, or arm around you; catching you alone for a quick kiss; the explicit proposition backed by threat of losing your job; and forced sexual relations."[7]

The Dilemma

Even though some definitions used in the workplace for sexual harassment are appropriate in education, additional definitions distinctive to the educational setting are needed.

In major universities, especially those that focus on research, the student may have very little opportunity for personal contact with a professor, let alone mentoring by him. Additionally, in most universities male faculty members far outnumber female faculty, especially in key positions of power, so female students may have little access to female faculty.

Faculty have an unusual amount of power because of the way academia functions. Many, many students want help and a very small number of faculty are available to give that help. A graduate student needs to have a faculty advisor as a guide through the university's academic maze and political structure. A good advisor gets a student into the right courses, helps make contacts with the right professors and researchers, helps with the shaping and development of the research project, and helps select a "friendly" thesis committee, so that ultimately the student will graduate.

Now suppose the faculty member is a person such as Phil, the sailboat sociologist. Because of his limited time with students, he selected a few of the brightest graduate students—particularly those female students who were most sexually interesting to him.

Once a female graduate student has started her program of study and finds she has a sexually harassing advisor, she may not be able to drop courses or change committee members without major repercussions, especially if she has invested years in collecting thesis data.

She may be forced to put up with sexual harassment for a long time, because leaving part way through graduate school means throwing away her academic career. Leaving will also certainly limit her options financially and professionally. Therefore, many women students put up with harassment, knowing eventually they will graduate and won't have to live with it anymore.

It Happens Too Often

A study done at an East Coast university, where 356 female graduate students responded, revealed that 60 percent of the sample had experienced at least one incident of sexual harassment by male faculty members.[8]

A 27-year-old single woman in a social science department gave an insight into the psychological pressure felt by graduate student women if a male professor starts the sexual harassment process.

"Throughout my first semester I experienced extensive social and sexual harassment from my advisor who was also my research supervisor, the teacher of two of my classes, and the faculty member under whom I served as a teaching assistant. Largely because of his harassment and lack of respect for me, I decided—very early in the semester—that I would switch advisors and work in someone else's lab.

"Because of all the power that he had over me and because I feared that he might use his power against me if I angered him, I waited until the end of the semester, after I received my grades, to tell him of my plans. I maintained a formal working relationship with him until that time.

"When I informed him (very tactfully) that I wanted to work in another lab, he became enraged—yelled at me, insulted me. Shortly thereafter, he talked with the faculty member (X) that he thought I was planning to work for—a conversation which was conveyed to me by a grad student who inadvertently overheard it.

"My former advisor told X that if I worked under him, his (X's) reappointment and tenure would be more difficult.

"A few days later, X—who had previously been actively recruiting me—told me that I should work under someone else, without telling me why.

"About a week after this incident, my former advisor called a meeting of the faculty to discuss my 'case.' He told the other faculty that I was not interested in research and that I should be kicked out of the program immediately. (I received all A's and A/B's my first semester from him!) Fortunately, the faculty did not act upon his recommendation and I managed, with difficulty, to switch to another lab. The trauma I experienced throughout this episode is beyond description. My career—my entire life—was in jeopardy."[9]

Women Fear Reporting Harassment

Although a high number of female graduate students experience sexual harassment and feel extremely negative about it, they also feel intimidated about filing a formal complaint. In fact, a study at Harvard University found that 14 out of 15 women with serious harassment incidents did not file a formal complaint because they feared reprisals and 50 percent of the women did not believe the university would take them seriously.[10]

In a study done at Sangamon State University, women commented on how they felt about sexual harassment:

☐ 74 percent felt angry
☐ 56.4 percent were embarrassed

☐ 28.5 percent felt intimidated

☐ only 1.5 percent felt flattered

These statistics are a clear indication that women do not enjoy these experiences.[11]

Typically, women feel a great deal of insecurity about themselves and the value of their work, as well as about the professors and the academic setting.

One graduate student said, "What was it that I did that led him to believe I was interested in him in anything but a professional sense? I am quite outgoing and talkative; could that be interpreted wrongly? I realized how utterly vulnerable I was in a situation like this.

"He is an immensely powerful person with many contacts and if I insult him, he can harm me and my career in a hundred different ways. Everything that happened would be interpreted in his favor, if it ever became public. It would be said that I got my signals wrong, that he was just truly interested in helping me in my career.

"I realized that should he try to hurt my professional advancement as a result of this kind of situation, there would be no person or formal mechanism to [whom I could] carry my grievance, no person I could complain to that would have any real power to help me. I was left feeling frustrated and defenseless."[12]

It's no wonder that women are afraid to tell. For example, in an interview published in a student newspaper, the dean of students stated that no women student had ever complained to him about being propositioned by male professors. In the same article the university president stated that he had no evidence of anything like that going on. Yet a faculty member at the same institution commented, "To be a teacher is to be a person with power. It is difficult to ignore the admiration many of your students feel about you, and I admit that I have used this power for selfish means."[13]

Help for Reducing Sexual Harassment

Students have tried several approaches to discourage sexual harassment, such as redirecting the conversation to educational topics if the professor started to talk about his personal life. Some women found it helpful to bring a friend with them, even if the friend just sat outside the professor's office. Frequently students deliberately left the door open and took a seat a safe distance from the professor.

Students also found it helpful to mention their boyfriend or husband by name. Sometimes they referred to a boyfriend, even when they didn't have one.

Mentioning a husband or a boyfriend seemed to be a helpful tactic, but a number of women in the Berkeley study said they felt it was still a compromise. They wished they could have been more direct and spoken to the professor about his sexual harassment.

Frequently, women tried the avoidance tactic. They would not hang around after class, never attend any of the harassing professor's open office hours, never speak to him alone. And some even went as far as to change advisors or majors.

Unfortunately, the very professors they avoided were the people who held the powerful keys to mentoring, advancement, casual learning and future career potential. So while these women were protecting themselves at the moment, they also felt they were cutting off some of their current learning potential and future career opportunities.[14]

Women are no longer in a powerless position if sexual harassment occurs. On most campuses clear policies are in place against sexual harassment with procedures for the voicing of complaints. But women *must* come forward to stop the problem.

Guidelines for Colleges and Universities

Many colleges and universities during the eighties began to put policies in place to define sexual harassment, giving examples of typical attitudes that will not be tolerated and suggesting the consequences of sexual harassment.

The University of Wisconsin at Madison has described in their guidelines four kinds of sexual harassment:
□ trading sexual favors for evaluations or grades
□ repeated or flagrant sexual advances
□ demeaning verbal or other expressive behavior in an instructional setting
□ demeaning verbal or expressive behavior in a noninstructional setting[15]

The Madison guidelines, however, were criticized by students and faculty because they were not specific and created loopholes.

The University of Iowa issued a sweeping policy about the relationship between faculty and students. The policy states, "The university will view it as unethical if faculty members engage in amorous relations with students enrolled in their classes or subject to their supervision, even when both parties appear to have consented to the relationship."[16]

More schools are releasing the names of the people who have been disciplined for sexual harassment. On some campuses where students feel that the issue has been kept too secret, they believe it's unfair to expose female students to potential mistreatment when a professor is a known sexual harasser. They argue that the university should make this information public so that student women will be able to choose other classes or other professors before getting embroiled in the sexual politics of education.

A new public records law in Hawaii is bringing great pressure to bear on the whole harassment issue. The state attorney general directed the state university to release the names of all state employees formerly charged with sexual harassment, even the cases that were pending or dismissed.[17]

The situation became so volatile in Hawaii that faculty and

staff unions filed suit and obtained a court injunction, ordering the university not to release the names of people charged with sexual harassment, especially those people whose cases were pending or had been dismissed. This action so enraged some of the students that they posted flyers identifying four professors who were sexual harassers.[18]

Clearly the situation is heating up on many campuses. Administrators will be hard pressed to keep the balance: preventing sexual harassment in all its forms, protecting the right to privacy and protecting people from unsubstantiated accusations.

The High Cost of Harassment to Women

A study done at the Work Clinic at the University of California Hospital in San Francisco shows that a disabling pattern is experienced by women who have been sexually harassed. Some of their symptoms include "chronic fatigue, loss of strength, various aches, weaknesses and pains. Others reacted with depression and symptoms of depression, such as sleeplessness and poor motivation. Still others reacted with psychological symptoms: nervousness, hypersensitivity, hostility, memory loss and feelings of victimization."[19]

Similar to women who are raped, sexually harassed women feel humiliated, degraded, shamed, embarrassed, cheap and angry. They rightly feel that professors who do this, and universities that allow it, are acting unprofessionally.

Women also bear the cost of self-doubt with thoughts such as:

☐ "Maybe I caused it to happen."

☐ "Maybe if I hadn't worn that red dress he wouldn't have harassed me."

☐ "Maybe, after all, it really is my fault."

Cost to the Institution

The obvious loss to the college or university is that students view some professors negatively, plus they feel that the administration doesn't care about the harassing situations. If the situations become intolerable, students will drop out or transfer to other institutions. So the cost to the institution is student retention and overall morale, not to mention damage to the primary purpose of the college or university—that of teaching. If true teaching, mentoring and learning cannot take place because of sexual harassment, the institution has paid too high a price for its failure to address the harassment problem.

Cost to Men

An additional cost of harassment that is often overlooked is the cost to the male harasser. Frequently, harassment is an indication of a deeper problem. The harasser may have a sexual addiction, may feel sexually insecure, may be experiencing marital problems, may be going through mid-life crisis, may be having difficulty with teenage children or may be feeling unfulfilled in his career.

When a harasser, such as Phil our sailing professor, is unchecked in his harassment, the real problems are ignored and the opportunity for emotional and spiritual help for the person is blocked. Sometimes it's helpful to view harassment as a call for help: "Please, catch me." "Please stop me." Since it is extremely difficult for men to ask for help, sometimes a foolish act of sexual harassment sets into motion the changes that he is unable or unwilling to make on his own.

What's the Answer?

The solution for the university has to come from many directions:

☐ carefully worded policy statements
☐ clear procedures for handling complaints
☐ punishment of harassers
☐ student awareness of harassment issues

☐ employment and promotion of more women faculty

Changing the gender balance in a college faculty tends to raise men's respect for women and hold in check the incidences of harassment.

Estelle Ramey talks about her own experience in academia. She landed a prize job on the faculty of a large university after she finished medical school. But forty years later at a school reunion she asked her old mentor, who was the chairman of the department, why he chose her over the hundreds of male graduates.

He told her that she was the smartest in the class and that she was ambitious and hardworking. "And you know," he added, "you were nice to look at."

Professor Ramey smiled at her old professor and mentor and thanked him. But she wondered within herself, *What if he had told me this at the time?*

"It would have reinforced my uneasiness as the only woman in the science department," she says. "At nineteen, twenty, or twenty-five, my self-image was so fragile. I had to be reinforced all the time."[20]

Sexual harassment in education is too costly to everyone involved; good solutions must be worked at and achieved.

6
Sexual Harassment in Religion

Mark Thompson had been a minister in the Midwest for more than fifteen years. He had counseled hundreds of people and could read them very well. As he watched Sylvia walk into his office for her first counseling appointment, he felt two opposing impressions. His first casual assessment of her drew an image of depression. Her face looked tired; dark circles ringed her eyes. She walked slowly, with shoulders slumped and head sagging. Her hair was combed, but that was all. She had on only a little makeup; her dress was not a complimentary color nor did it fit well.

The second strong impression Pastor Thompson felt was that underneath all the depression was a very beautiful woman. Her perfect facial structure, blue eyes, bright teeth, petite nose and gentle lips, weren't totally masked by her despondency. And he couldn't help noticing that the rest of her body was extremely attractive under her ill-fitting clothes.

Sylvia, in her late twenties, was employed as a dental lab technician and lived alone. She attended church frequently but always was on the fringe. She never seemed to be able to connect with people, although the pastor noticed that the young men in the singles group were often interested in her.

Pastor Thompson invited Sylvia to have a seat while he sat in his chair behind his desk. "Now, what can I do for you?"

She hesitated, looking down at the floor. Finally, after some minutes of awkward silence, she said, "I have trouble getting along with people."

Bit by bit, the agonizing story began to unfold. By the time she was twelve years old she had the body of a fully developed woman. The boys, especially the older ones, gave her a lot of attention. She was glad to hang around with them because it showed the girls her age that at least somebody wanted to be her friend.

But it wasn't just friendship the boys wanted. Soon she was being exploited by one boy after another. She hated being used that way; she knew that the football players all talked about her. But at least they were paying attention to her.

There was no stability for Sylvia at home. Her parents were constantly battling. Her father was an alcoholic, causing the marriage to teeter on the brink of divorce.

Just before Sylvia was fourteen, her father came home drunk one evening. The house was empty since his wife was at work and the two older boys were out for the evening.

Sylvia's father started crying, telling her how bad he felt because things weren't going well at work and her mother didn't love him. In fact, nobody loved him.

In his drunken stupor he put his arms around Sylvia asking, "You love me, don't you? You love me?"

She tried to reassure him that she loved him, when suddenly his mood began to change. He stopped crying and spoke in an angry tone: "Then show me that you love me. All around town

I hear that you show the high-school boys how much you love them. Show me!"

He pushed her to the living room floor, ripped off her clothes and raped her.

Sheep's Clothing

Pastor Thompson felt a deep pity for this young woman sitting before him. As she began to cry, almost involuntarily he got up from his seat, came around to her chair and put his arms around her.

As he stood there comforting her, an evil thought crossed his mind. "If all of these other men have had sex with Sylvia, why don't I? After all, I can truly love her."

The intercom clicked on; it was Pastor Thompson's secretary, telling him that his next appointment was waiting. Pastor Thompson told Sylvia, "I have to let you go now, but I want to see you again."

She responded, "You're so kind and caring. I know you're busy, and I'm very grateful for the time."

Pastor Thompson looked at his desk calendar and suggested they meet the following Wednesday for a longer session. He didn't tell Sylvia that Wednesday afternoon his secretary would not be at work. Nor did he tell her that he had crossed a line in his mind. Over the next several months he was going to repeatedly use her trust and the power of his position to have sex with her.

His Power/Her Power

Sylvia is a classic case of sexual harassment in a religious setting. All the ingredients were there to make it happen.

Abuse of power was one of the main issues here. Sylvia had no power, because she had a boundary problem. She had felt powerless since she was a child. Men constantly used their power to exploit her sexually. She hoped that men would be benefactors—people who could help her in life. But she discovered that to get their help, she had to give in to their sexual harassment.

Pastor Thompson possessed a great deal of power. He had established himself as a respected community person, a leader in the church and the mouthpiece of God. He was a wise and caring man in the eyes of many people, especially Sylvia.

Even though she told her minister the terrible stories of how she had been sexually abused by her father, the neighborhood boys, and man after man in her twenties, he didn't really hear the pain of her story. His caring demeanor didn't stop him from giving in to his primal desires and joining in the exploitation.

I'm Not Harassing

Pastor Thompson saw a woman he could manipulate for his own sexual pleasure. He used his position of power to control Sylvia and set her up for sex.

He asked the questions and steered the direction of the counseling sessions. *He* got her to give him detailed information about each of her sexual experiences. *He* asked what the men did, how they touched her, how she felt, how she reacted, what gave her pleasure even in the midst of her pain.

The more Sylvia talked about her sexual experiences, the more aroused Pastor Thompson became. Strangely, he began to believe that Sylvia talked about her sex life because *she* wanted to. He totally blocked from his mind the fact that *he,* with his power as a pastoral counselor, was steering the counseling discussions into these graphic sexual areas.

Most sexual harassers do not believe that they are harassing anyone. Certainly Pastor Thompson didn't believe that he was harassing Sylvia. If questioned, he would have responded that he was simply trying to get the full understanding of her story so he could help her.

Sexual harassers also do not understand that their perception is distorted. In Pastor Thompson's skewed mind, he honestly believed that she was talking about sex because, secretly, she wanted to have sex with him.

A vicious delusionary cycle started with Sylvia in a "power-down" situation and Pastor Thompson in a "power-up" situation. He got her to talk about sex, which in turn fed and twisted his thinking so that he actually believed she wanted to have sex with him. What Sylvia really wanted was for this wise and caring man to help her become a whole person and to recover her sense of dignity. She needed him to steer her on a track toward a positive self-image and a sense of cleanness before God. But she got none of these.

The Easy Trap

In *The Problem Clergymen Don't Talk About,* the author cites Gordon Legge, a local church minister and counselor for several counseling centers, who reports that sexual problems between ministers and their congregations are not uncommon.

He quotes a psychiatrist: "Whenever two people work very closely together toward a common goal with at least fair success, as a minister does with his parishioner, or a doctor with his patient, feelings of camaraderie and warmth almost inevitably arise between them. When the two people are of opposite sex and not too different in background, these warm feelings will almost always assume a sexual cast."[1]

A doctoral thesis done at Fuller Theological Seminary, entitled "The Hazards of the Ministry," revealed that 37 percent of the ministers surveyed confessed to inappropriate sexual behavior with someone in their congregation. Additionally, 12 percent confessed to having had a sexual affair with at least one of their parishioners during their years of ministry.[2]

These statistics are self-reported by the ministers. Plus, 5 percent did not answer the sexual section. Therefore, the numbers could be higher, with perhaps over 40 percent of ministers being sexually inappropriate. In addition, as we have seen in the dating chapter, men grossly underestimate whether what they are doing is sexual harassment. So, again, the statistics are likely much higher.

How the Mighty Have Fallen

In the late eighties and early nineties, scandal after scandal occurred in religious circles with such notables as Jim Bakker and Jimmy Swaggart, both of national television fame, and many others. Each used women sexually for their own indulgence.

In the past few years it seems that almost every week we hear of another prominent pastor who has resigned from ministry because of being sexually involved with parishioners. One national radio program collapsed and went off the air when it was disclosed that two previous speakers on the program, both highly respected ministers, had been sexually involved with their church members and had been forced to resign.

One Catholic priest, James R. Porter, achieved dreadful national fame when it was disclosed that he had sexually abused dozens of children in several states over the years of his ministry.[3] Other priests and bishops are also being charged with sexual misconduct.

The Catholic church was shocked by the resignation of Robert Sanchez, Archbishop of the Santa Fe Diocese in Albuquerque, New Mexico. He admitted having affairs with several parishioners and protecting several of his priests who had a history of sexually abusing children.[4]

The United Church of Canada has an internal task force which recommended the church develop a code of ethics for its ministers because of the "horrific proportions" of sexual harassment in the church.[5]

Gordon Legge quotes John White as he talks about what a real man is: "A [spiritually and emotionally healthy] man is in control of his sexuality." White believes that men are having a great deal of difficulty with sexuality today. They are failing to live up to their own standards of sexual morality, and the new sexual definitions of men and women. Their hormones and confusion are more than they can handle.

Legge says, "Whenever White asks men who attend his workshops to step forward if they are having trouble dealing with sexual sin, anywhere from a third to a half come forward for prayer." White says, "It shows me the time is right to deal with it among Christian leaders."[6]

Power Changes the Situation
People in religious power positions, such as pastors, priests and counselors, need to keep two facts in mind:
☐ Sexual overtures initiated by them are legally and morally wrong.
☐ Even if there is no sexual intercourse, any sexual behavior—verbal or physical—will be viewed as harassment.

Sometimes clergymen have excused themselves by saying, "I was not sexually harassing her or exploiting her—we were in love."

The power situation changes the dynamics of "why" these two people got romantically involved. They are not two equals who happened to meet at a party and started a dating relationship. Rather, one person in a power position is using power for personal sexual pleasure.

Frequently, pastors and church leaders who confess to having sexual thoughts about parishioners feel it's okay as long as they don't actually have sexual intercourse.

For example, Ralph has been a deacon in a number of churches, served on church boards, taught various classes, directed musical programs and is a powerful leader in his denomination as well as his local church. He adamantly believes that sexual intercourse outside of marriage is wrong. Frequently, he has gone on record against the permissiveness of society. Yet he uses his power position and the church setting to harass women.

His favorite trick is to greet women on Sunday morning with a "holy hug and kiss." The church he attends is very warm and caring. So Ralph exploits that characteristic by greeting woman after woman with a full-body hug, pressing her breasts firmly against his chest and kissing her on the neck.

Another of his tricks is to come up behind a woman and slip his hands underneath her arms to hug her just below her breasts. It's interesting that Ralph never hugs men. He only shakes their hand. He justifies that by saying he wouldn't want anyone to think he is a homosexual.

But Would It Be "Christian" to Object?
Ralph gives women the creeps. They want to protest, but they feel that speaking up would not be "Christian." The women decide not to say anything because "After all, Ralph is a leading deacon and he probably doesn't mean anything by it."

But this is flat-out sexual harassment, and the truth of the matter is that Ralph *does* mean something by it. He's constantly looking for sexual targets. He uses his power to gratify his own addiction. To a few who have confronted him, he justifies what he does by saying, "I'm just overly sexed, and my wife doesn't give me enough sexual attention."

Ralph believes what he does is harmless because he is not involved in intercourse. Ralph is *absolutely dead wrong!* The church leaders should speak out against this conduct and specifically confront Ralph. Sexual harassment is defined the same way in a religious setting as in any other setting. If a person uses power, words or touch for his own personal sexual gratification—sexual harassment has taken place.

In *Sex in the Forbidden Zone,* Peter Rutter points out the damaging misuse of power over women by men in leadership.[7]

One of his examples is that of a personal assistant to a seminary dean.

The dean of the seminary, Rev. Clifton, told his assistant, Ruth, that their sexual relationship was part of her training. It must be kept secret as proof of her spiritual development and commitment to the church.

Ruth had begun studying at a small midwestern seminary. She was then twenty-one, and Rev. Clifton was a married man with five children.

She said, "When he offered me a job as his personal assistant, requiring intimate daily contact, I remember getting a sick feeling in my stomach about my giving him so much power over my life. But he was offering me the fulfillment of a dream I had always had of a very special kind of recognition, so I pushed away my feeling that it was wrong."

Ruth began a five-year sexual relationship. Since Rev. Clifton was a nationally prominent religious educator, he demanded complete secrecy and was concerned about his reputation.

Even though Ruth wanted to serve the church, the affair pushed her away from her life goals. "I felt total isolation," she said, "because I could not speak to anyone about this relationship. If I only could have had more trust in myself."

Finally she stopped the relationship when he started having sexual relationships with other women. But she continued to maintain silence about his sexual affairs. She was eventually ordained by him, but it was a hollow experience. Ruth is now thirty, and she feels emotionally cut off from the religious community to which she felt called.

She said, "My relationship with Rev. Clifton was so destructive not primarily because of my sexual enslavement, but because he further decimated my trust in myself and deepened my own self-hatred. I violated myself by attempting to trust him more than myself. . . . I can't tell you how painful it is for me to look straight on at how many years of my life sank into that black mire, and really to know that I'm not over it."

Dr. Rutter explains why women like Ruth succumb to psychic paralysis when a moment of sexual touching crosses their sexual boundary:

The result is paralysis—of action, judgment, feeling, and voice. The cultural messages encouraging passivity, the personal wounds from her family that have shown her there is no protective boundary, the hope that someone will treat her differently all come together as an overwhelming flood at the moment the man touches her. This paralysis can last for minutes, hours, days, and sometimes years. In the meantime, the man has proceeded with his sexual scenario.

At this point, a woman can completely shut down her feelings, dissociating herself from the body that is acting sexually. This split creates a state called 'psychic numbing,' a term that was first used to describe the effect on people who are completely powerless in the face of overwhelming catastrophe, such as concentration camp internment.[8]

Things to Remember in a Religious Setting

In most religious groups there is a condition of closeness, caring, praying for each other and mutual support. This type of setting can be an open invitation to the sexual harasser under the guise of religious caring.

If you feel creepy about the way someone looks at you, touches you, comments or jokes, or if you wonder about the squeeze of the arm or an uncomfortable hug, pat or kiss, don't ignore that feeling. It's God's internal warning sign to you that something is wrong.

Don't excuse the action, the look or the comment just because you are in a religious setting or the person is a religious person. What we wouldn't tolerate in a work setting is frequently tolerated in a church setting—but it should not be.

Recently Sally and I were sitting in church and I was at the end of the aisle. The service was about to begin as a couple came over to greet us. Their marriage is not good, and the woman has frequently violated boundaries with her adult children. She told Sally that she was glad to see her looking so well and able to be at church. (Sally has been battling cancer.) Then, just as she was about to leave—and with her husband standing meekly behind her—she bent down and gave me a wet, sloppy kiss on the neck.

I was shocked.

She quickly turned and walked away as the organ started to play the first hymn. Perhaps she knew that I wouldn't jump up and confront her just as the service was starting. I felt yukky! I kept rubbing my neck, hoping I could rub this feeling away.

Several times during the afternoon I commented to Sally about how awful it felt to have this woman kiss me in this way. She got away with violating my boundaries under the guise of the caring setting of the church.

Actions to Consider in a Religious Setting

All the guidelines we have given earlier for confronting sexual harassment at work also apply in a religious setting. We want to encourage you to listen carefully to your feelings and follow the guidelines you'll find in chapter eight. There is a possibility that you will experience low-level sexual harassment in the church because it is an environment where people are more open to each other.

If your feelings send up a warning flag—if you feel shame or fear, for example, or if anger starts to rise within you—let those feelings help you to take action. You don't have to feel embarrassed to confront someone just because it's a church.

Say to the person on the spot or after the service, "I would rather that you not hug me again. I feel very uncomfortable." If the actions continue, you need to warn the person that you are going to alert a church official. Churches are increasingly sensitized today to the need of protecting their people from sexual harassers.

Another important action is to share your feelings with a friend. Choose a person who will believe you and validate your feelings rather than someone who is going to say, "You're imagining it," or "How could that happen? This is a church!" Let your friend or your small group know how angry you felt. Also, share the other feelings you may have experienced such as shame, fear or self-blame.

When your experience is validated by another person, that will help dissipate your negative emotion. And it will help you see that the problem is not yours but rather the sexual harasser's.

The Lost Bike

In the film "The Coward of the County," Kenny Rogers played the role of a small-town preacher at the beginning of World War II. One Sunday morning he preached on the Ten Commandments. As he paced around the pulpit, he told a humorous story of an old-time preacher who had his bicycle stolen. This left the preacher with no way of getting around town to make his calls.

He was complaining to one of the church deacons, and the deacon suggested that he preach on the Ten Commandments. "When you get to the section about 'Thou shall not steal,' really pound the pulpit and drive the point home. It'll make the thief feel guilty and return your bike."

So the next Sunday the preacher did preach on the Ten Commandments. After he had finished the sermon, the deacon said to him, "Well, Pastor, you preached on the Ten Commandments, but you didn't emphasize 'Thou shall not steal.' Why not? Don't you want your bicycle back?"

The pastor looked at the deacon rather sheepishly and said, "You know, it's a funny thing—when I was preparing that message on the Ten Commandments, I got to the section about 'Thou shall not commit adultery,' and I remembered where I left my bicycle."

In the movie, everyone in the church laughed at the story. But it's not a laughing matter. Sexual harassment is a tragic fact of life, and it doesn't become right when it is done by a religious person! Both men and women need to take courageous steps to eliminate sexual harassment from churches, synagogues and other religious institutions and activities.

7
Why Do Women Put Up with It?

Y ou may ask, "Why do women put up with these disgusting behaviors?" There are as many reasons for tolerating
sexual harassment as there are harassed women, of course.

Perhaps some women were raised in homes or are in marriages where boundaries are not respected. They hardly notice
that someone is intruding into their space. All they feel is a dull
unpleasantness and a desire to avoid this person.

Many women are not sure what is appropriate behavior.
Low-level sexual harassment, such as a borderline compliment
or a touch on the back, is especially baffling to both men and
women. A woman will frequently follow the lead of a man,
especially a more powerful man, letting him decide what is right
or wrong.

Many women have been taught that the Bible says to be
submissive to all males. As a result, it is difficult for them to
say no to any man.

An astounding number of women put up with sexual harassment on the job, on dates, in marriage, education, the military, religion—because society has convinced them that they have asked for it. The woman thinks to herself, "Maybe my blouse is too tight, or my skirt is too short, or maybe I smiled too much. Whatever it is, I must have done something to lead him on."

The four most common reasons we have heard why women tolerate the humiliation of sexual harassment are:

☐ I need the money from this job.
☐ Men have the power.
☐ I hope it won't happen again.
☐ It does more harm than good to complain.

"I Need the Money"
Marie took a job as an executive in the Financial Trade Association. She explained, "I was recently separated, my husband was unemployed and the first of our five children was starting college. I needed the money."

She continued, "The second week on the job a woman was raped in the parking garage we used, and we were discussing the need for precautions. A vice president stood in the middle of the office and smilingly said, 'Sexual harassment, I love it.' I remember the chill I felt as everyone laughed. The remark was made in the presence of other male executives, surrounded by female support staff and me. I knew then the environment was going to be hostile."

Marie went on to say, "Women in that office were supposed to be pretty and pleasant. Sexual affairs were routine and comments about women's bodies were a daily occurrence."

Many women don't change jobs because they believe harassment is everywhere—and they need the income.

"Men Have the Power"
Marie has since gone to another job, but she talks about her

former employer, who was a harasser: "Our world is small, and in one part of my world he is still there: a powerful man who controls resources, who has national organizations that potentially influence my work."

She continues, "Only white men who hold power could be so naive as to ask why a woman would stay in touch with a man or a place where she had been subjected to verbal harassment. Women do not have the luxury of cutting themselves off from men who hold power in our professions, and I don't know one woman with the professional power of my ex-employer."

She explains that she understands why Anita Hill did not blow the whistle earlier and why she tolerated the harassment at all. She says, "The Judiciary Committee's dismissal of Anita Hill's story is about men not understanding what it is like not to have power. Clarence Thomas is a man who held and holds power in Ms. Hill's profession. Until this week, he was certain to hold one of the most powerful positions in her world."[1]

We can get a better understanding of what sexual harassment means if we understand the power issues involved. The harasser is typically the one who has more power than the one being harassed. The unequal power situation is set up so that the one with less power must please the supervisor or administrator who has control over the job situation.

When harassment occurs, the power is naturally weighted toward the one in leadership. The teeter-totter is tilted so that sexual irritation and torment are almost automatically accepted by the person with no power.

Another part of the picture is the "power high" felt by the harasser. A subtle victory is won if the harassment is not rejected. To many men, the unrebuffed flirtatious comment or touch is as exhilarating as closing a big business deal. It's like the salesmen who makes his first sale to a company who is likely to be a repeat buyer. The harasser not only feels the thrill of the first "victory," but he knows many more will follow.

"I Hope It Won't Happen Again"

The woman who experiences the first low-level harassment from her supervisor—a comment about her clothes, an arm around her shoulder, a wink or a stare—begins to play tapes in her head that generally help her to ignore her feelings. These mental messages clearly acknowledge her lower power situation. She hopes it won't happen again.

She says things to herself such as:

□ He's only trying to be friendly.

□ I'm just getting started in this job. No one else has said anything bad about this man.

□ His comment that I am a good-looking woman and that he especially liked me in my sweater outfit was really just appreciating the fact that I dress nicely for work.

The woman who begins to play mental messages like these is setting herself up for the next harassment. But she says, "He has power over my job, and I need the money." So she fantasizes, "It probably won't happen again."

"It Does More Harm Than Good to Complain"

Part of the answer to the question of why women put up with harassment is the longstanding pattern of nothing being done when sexual harassment is exposed. Frequently, only lip service is given to the accusation.

Or, as in the case of the Newport Beach police oficers, punishment to the harasser is only a mockery. After the four women making accusations against the officers were given a small out-of-court settlement, the two male officers who committed the crimes were allowed to retire with full retirement salaries and other lucrative benefits, including having their attorneys' fees paid. Any record of the allegations against them has been removed from their files. Many area residents are enraged that these two men avoided a court case, in which they probably would have been found guilty. In addition, they can walk away with the same financial benefits as if they had honorably served the city until retirement age.[2]

In a survey done by Working Women United, 70 percent of the women who had been harassed ignored the harassing. However, the harassing did not stop just because they ignored it. In more than half the cases, the women who did complain through established channels reported that no action resulted. One-third of the women who complained said that they experienced negative repercussions such as increased work loads, complaints about the quality of their work, reprimands and poor personnel reports.[3]

Understanding the power issue helps us see why the numbers vary so widely between accusations and disciplinary actions. For example, the United States Office of Personnel Management found that, in a two-year period, four out of twelve federal agencies had disciplined a total of only fourteen workers for engaging in sexual harassment. In the same study they had surveyed 23,000 federal employees and found that 42 percent of the women reported having been victims of sexual harassment during that same two-year period. *Yet only fourteen people were reprimanded or penalized.*

The study further went on to project, using their 42 percent figure, that it was likely during this two-year period that over 300,000 female federal employees were victims of sexual harassment. In addition, 9,000 probably experienced rape or sexual assault. Yet the reported cases are an extremely small percentage of the women actually being harassed.[4]

In *Sexual Harassment of Working Women: A Case of Sex Discrimination,* Catherine MacKinnon said all of the studies on sexual harassment she had reviewed indicated a majority of females object to harassment. Women neither want to be harassed at work nor find it flattering. "To say that women want to be harassed is as foolish as saying that they want to be raped," MacKinnon asserts.[5]

Responsibilities of Employers

The old ways in which men and women related in the workplace are totally obsolete. Behaviors that used to be accepted are now considered crude or demeaning and legally are considered a "hostile work environment." Even such simple things as calling another employee "honey" or a friendly touch on a woman's upper arm rather than a handshake are sexual innuendoes to many women.

In an article entitled "Employers Urged to Enact Sex Harassment Policies," the author reported an interview with Laurie J. Bilik who is an associate professor at the New York-based College of Insurance. Bilik said that the 1991 Civil Rights Act has granted monetary awards for sexual harassment that were previously unavailable.

The act now allows for punitive damages stemming from sexual harassment and discrimination. Employers with 15 to 100 employees can face punitive damages of $15,000. Employers with 101 to 200 employees can face up to $100,000 in damages. Companies with 201 to 500 employees can be hit with up to $200,000.

According to Ms. Bilik, punitive damages are not the only losses that can occur as a result of sexual harassment. Other losses can include low morale, low productivity and high employee turnover.

She said, "Since what constitutes sexual harassment is often in the eyes of the beholder, employers had better take a claim seriously. The legal questions of what the standards of acceptable behavior should be and from whose perspective [they are to be judged] are still being thrashed out."[6]

Lifelong Harasser

Donald was a hard-driving workaholic who kept being promoted until he was vice president of personnel in a national insurance company. His task was to oversee the personnel needs for approximately three hundred people in the home office where he was stationed, as well as to supervise other personnel managers in several other cities.

Don had started out as an insurance salesman. He was aggressive, following up on leads and making frequent contacts in clients' homes.

It was during this phase of his insurance career that Don first got into trouble. He started making frequent calls on some of the female clients in their homes at times when their husbands would not be there.

On the surface, it appeared he was just coming by to collect the premium payment. But Don liked to touch people. He had a programmed escalation of touches for women, from handshakes to touches on the arm or knee to an arm around the shoulder—and, finally, full-body hugs as he would say, "You're one of my *very* special customers."

He was looking for a vulnerable woman who would open the door to him. Then he ran into Rita. She politely shook hands, but as he started his maneuvers of the full-body hug, she became inwardly very angry.

She didn't say anything, but she called the insurance office as soon as he left. The office manager listened to her complaint and when Don returned to the office, the manager said, "You'll have to watch it with Rita. She's really angry. In fact, she even thinks you're trying to come on to her sexually." The manager and Don laughed and the matter was dropped.

Mid-Life Distortion
By the time Don got into his forties, he was an area manager and he was going through a mid-life crisis. He didn't feel the insurance company was recognizing his abilities. His marriage seemed dull and stale. And he began to feel "old."

Unfortunately, he started to share his feelings with Heidi, a twenty-eight-year-old single woman who worked as a secretary in the office. Heidi enjoyed helping people, so she listened to Don, hoping that she might be an encouragement.

As Heidi helped Don, he took it as a sign that she was interested in him romantically. So he started making moves—coffee together, inviting her to lunch and asking her if she could stay later to work on a project at the office. Don tried to keep her "hooked" by telling her one or two juicy tidbits, each time they talked, about how depressed he felt.

One evening, after a late-night stay at the office, Don helped Heidi into her coat. As she put it on, he turned her around toward him and started buttoning her coat down the front. As he got to the second button, he pulled the astonished Heidi to himself and kissed her on the lips.

Heidi stepped back and stood with her mouth open. She didn't know what was happening. She was not at all interested in this man romantically—really not even as a friend. Her only concern was to help, the same way she'd care for a stray kitten. She was in shock. She wondered what to do. When she told Marie, her roommate, Marie said, "Looks like you can do one of two things. You can talk to your regional manager or to Don himself, and you'll probably get fired if you do either. Or you can just quietly quit your job and move to something else." Heidi decided to quit.

The next day she told Don that she was quitting. Don was jolted as he watched Heidi walk out the door with her box of belongings. He followed her and asked, "What happened? Why did you change so much from last night?" Don saw it as Heidi's problem, not his.

In a Jam

Now Don is in his middle fifties and his company has recently enacted a policy statement against sexual harassment. He learned that his job would be to enforce a harassment-free workplace.

During the two days of training about how to eliminate sexual harassment, he came to realize that many of the ways he talked to and touched women were *legally* sexual harassment. Now he was on the spot. He was supposed to make sure nobody harassed; yet all of these unresolved issues were in his own life. If he didn't enforce the company policy, he'd lose his job. If he did enforce it, he might lose his male friends, or they might say, "You do the same things!"

And what if, by some strange chance, Rita or Heidi or someone working in the office now should accuse him? Don was in a tough spot. For the first time, he realized that during his entire insurance career he had "legally" been a sexual harasser.

The Manager's Own Lifestyle
Sometimes the reason that supervisors do not effectively handle sexual harassment cases is that they are faced with their own harassing behavior. Their personal harassment problems get in the way of solving these cases and eliminating sexual inappropriateness.

Frequently a manager who has his own sexual harassment issues will project the blame onto the victim. Here are some of the poor reasons managers give for allowing harassment to continue:

☐ It's really just a personality conflict raised by a prudish, unhappy person.

☐ Maybe it's a social problem outside of the office.

☐ This seems to be a power play to undermine management.

☐ If I ignore it, the situation will resolve itself.

☐ Disgruntled employees file these complaints to take the spotlight off their poor performance.

☐ I've behaved in a similar manner—it's not that bad!

☐ Sex is embarrassing to talk about.

☐ I don't like conflict.

☐ I could make the situation worse if I mess with this.

☐ I won't get support from my management.

☐ I am, or the sexual harasser is, about to retire.

☐ It is easier for me to ignore this sexual harassment than to enforce corrective action.

Management personnel must understand that if they were sued for not taking action to stop sexual harassment, it is doubtful that any of the above reasons would provide them with an adequate defense.

If women know that they will be protected—or at least vindicated when sexually harassed—they won't put up with it anymore. Men will have to change.

But what if you are being harassed? You don't want to lose your job and you're afraid to say anything to your harasser. You feel trapped!

What's the answer? The next chapter gives the practical coaching you need to get the harasser off your back.

8
Guidelines for the Harassed Person

Amy was a tender, naive girl, still finding her way in the work world, when one of the salesmen in the small company where she worked began to pay special attention to her.

Amy knew Frank was married. So why would he be bringing her flowers? She thought, "Maybe he takes turns doing that for all the women in the office." But after a few weeks she realized she was the only one receiving special gifts. Frank continually hung around her desk; she tried not to offend him while she went on with her work.

Then he began to ask to drive her home. She always patiently replied, "I have my car here."

Amy became confused and unsure of herself. Something told her that Frank's behavior was wrong, but she didn't want to hurt his feelings. Alone in her bed at night, she felt ashamed and didn't really know why. She had never been alone with Frank, except once when he caught her in the hall and tried to kiss her.

Before too long, Trudy and some of the other office women began to warn Amy. Trudy had been Frank's target before Amy came to the company. He had started out just as persistently with Trudy, but Trudy wasn't unsure or timid about his overtures. She didn't care if she embarrassed him. He never did take subtle rejection signs, so she became very blunt, telling him she would file charges with management if he didn't stop harassing her. Finally he backed off.

When Trudy noticed he had started to make moves on Amy, she watched quietly for a few days. She could see that Amy didn't know how to handle the situation. So Trudy took action. She told Amy what was happening. With tactful questions she helped Amy see that Frank's behavior was out of line. Trudy and the other women volunteered to protect Amy if Frank followed her at lunchtime or at the end of the day. Amy started to realize that these women were her allies and she wouldn't be wrong to defend herself against Frank.

Crucial Principles

If Amy had possessed a healthy self-esteem and appropriate boundaries, she could have avoided the hassles with Frank from the start.

Here are five guidelines for any harassment situation:

1. Generally speaking, harassment needs to be addressed *when it takes place* or very soon after the experience. To say nothing communicates to the harasser that you are fair game. Amy experienced unnecessary emotional trauma and repeated sexual "hits" from Frank because she hadn't thought through her own feelings about the harassment. Because Amy was uncertain, she was unable to clearly say "No!" when Frank first started his moves.

It's okay to say immediately, "I don't like that." You don't have to be harassed several times before you act.

2. Take *small, clear actions* at first to correct the harassment.

Escalate your responses if the harasser doesn't change his behavior.

For example, a supervisor may say to a woman, "You're a great addition to the office, I like your work—and I also like the way you fill out that sweater." Immediately, the woman needs to respond gently but firmly, "Your comment about my clothes makes me feel very, very uncomfortable. I'm glad for praise about my work, but not about my body." Then she needs to make a note in her own file of the date and time this happened, exactly what the supervisor said and what she said in response.

If harassment happens again, she needs to prepare a written memo with a duplicate that she keeps. She should hand deliver the memo to the harasser, explaining in it that this is now the second time he has made a sexual remark to her, that she doesn't appreciate harassment and that she doesn't want these kinds of remarks to intrude in their working situation.

If a third incident occurs, she might ask for *informal intervention* from the personnel department or the Equal Employment Opportunities officer. She should not ask for a formal investigation yet. Let a third person informally carry the message to the perpetrator that the harassment is not appreciated and is against company policy. The warning should also be noted in the files of both the woman and the third-party intervener.

3. If all this fails to stop the harassment, *formal investigation and action* should be requested. The harassed woman is dealing with a person with a serious problem who is either unable or unwilling to change. The formal investigation is likely to be successful because she has a recorded history of the harassing events and the procedures followed in each event.

4. It's important, at the time of the request for informal third-party assistance or formal investigation, for the harassed woman to *express her fears about future retaliation*.

5. Six months to a year after the harassment has stopped, an outside observer should *evaluate* to see whether there has been any retaliation, such as negative reviews or job discrimination.

The Victims

Women must support each other when harassment occurs. Women staffers for *The Washington Post* talked about their sexual harassment experiences for an article entitled "Between the Sexes, Confusion at Work: Harassment Is Widespread and Its Effects Are Long-lasting."[1] Their frank discussion of the harassment they experienced in journalism was a direct result of the Clarence Thomas hearings.

Their combined assessment was, "Sexual harassment is one snapshot experience that binds working women together and separates them from male colleagues."

Abigail Trafford, the author of the article, said, "While there is confusion over what exactly constitutes sexual harassment, there is no confusion about how it feels. The memories are vivid; so are the shame, fear and despair."

Most women who experience sexual harassment are younger women whose careers are not established and whose self-images may not be fully developed. They are in a vulnerable position if a power move is initiated by a supervisor or mentor.

Trafford warns, "Sexual harassment, whether it's a crack about her breasts from the janitor or a leer from the vice-president of sales, reinforces the self-doubt with the notion that women don't really belong in the workplace."[2]

The *Washington Post* women shared several stories. One of the women worked for a man that kept pressuring her to go out with him and to sleep with him. She rebuffed him. Then he gave her a poor performance rating in her annual evaluation. She never reported it.

Harassment was illustrated by another *Post* staffer whose coworker, senior to her, kept propositioning her and making sexual remarks. She told him to stop, but he continued to bother her. She found that he was doing the same to another female employee. They both went to their supervisor to complain. The supervisor took the male coworker aside and told him to stop bothering the two women. The overt actions stopped, but tension increased and one of the women moved to another department.

Another staffer reported that she was "in the middle of the newsroom when an editor, who had been drinking, came up to her and thrust his head between her breasts. Stunned, she pushed him away and pretended nothing had happened. Her supervisor, who had seen the incident, complimented her on how well she handled it; the editor received no official reprimand."[3]

Good—Pretty—or "Pretty Good"?

A big problem for the woman who is sexually harassed by a mentor or person with career-helping potential is that she's not sure whether he thinks her work is good or her body is good.

One woman, speaking of her first boss and how excited she was to work on special projects with him, said it was natural for him to take her to lunch. And then one day he leaned over, took her hand, and said, "Let's have an affair."

She was devastated. She clearly told him no, but how was she to handle the doubts that now filled her mind? "What about the bonus he gave her, the glowing evaluation? Was it because she was competent or because she was pretty?"[4]

A Thorny Problem

Harassment is complicated to handle. Sometimes the best way to understand ourselves or other people and sexual harassment is to take a specific situation and imagine that we are one of the people and we need to make a decision. In the following story put yourself into the shoes of Jerry Tarkwell, real estate lending manager at Filmore Trust. Then put yourself into the shoes of Jill McNair, an associate in the same organization; Jerry is her boss.

Jerry Tarkwell called Jill's office because he needed a file immediately. But Jill was not at her desk, so he decided to run down to her office and get the file himself. When he got there, Jill was still not back, so he went in to see if he could quickly spot the file. It was right on top of a pile of folders.

As he picked it up, Jerry noticed an interoffice message that Jill had typed on her computer, which read:

"Can you walk me out again tonight? He's in today and I'm sure he'll be waiting for me. He leaned up against me when I was at the coffee machine this morning and whispered some disgusting stuff about how great he is in bed."

Jerry was shocked and disgusted. He decided to correct the situation by calling the department in charge of handling sexual harassment charges within the company.

When Jill returned, her secretary told her Jerry had come for the file. As she sat down at her desk, she was shocked to see that she had left her computer message there on the screen.

Just then the phone rang. Jerry wanted to see her. As she headed toward his office, her sick stomach told her he was going to ask about that message.

Jerry came right to the point. "I couldn't help but see the message on your computer, Jill. This is terrible. I called the equal employment office. Let's put a stop to it."

With eyes flashing, Jill attacked. "You had no right to read my personal E-mail, and you had no right to call EEO before talking to me. This is my personal problem, not yours, and I don't want this getting around. Do you have any idea what can happen to me and to my career if people find out about this?"

Jerry tried to calm Jill by explaining that no one would have to know: she could write a letter and the EEO would take care of it.

"Don't you understand?" she seethed. "It would be his word against mine, and he's senior to me." She wished she hadn't let that slip. "I'm the one who's going to get hurt. If this gets investigated by EEO, everyone in this building could be questioned. I'll probably get transferred, and then I won't have a chance at promotion. And who'd want to work with me? Every man in the company would be afraid I'd report him if he so much as opened a door for me."

Jerry tried again to explain, but Jill responded angrily, "I won't have my privacy invaded. There's nothing you can do."

Jerry pleaded, "But it's a federal law! You don't have to take that kind of treatment. Besides, I have to report this. It's company policy."

Jill again exploded in anger as she headed for the door, "I've got too much at stake here. So just stay out of it, Jerry. I can take care of it myself."[5]

What Would You Do?

How would you feel if you were either of these two people? Would you have done anything differently? Was Jerry wrong in what he did or the way he did it? What about Jill? Did she overreact?

Harassment cases usually are complex. The incidents may include concrete actions or words or may be quite subjective. The answer to the question, "Has harassment taken place?" is largely an emotional one, given not by the perpetrator but by the person who has been harassed.

It is important to keep several factors in mind:

☐ Sexual harassers usually continue harassing until they are confronted.

☐ Frequently, if harassment is not dealt with strongly enough, the harasser simply shifts focus to another person.

☐ Sometimes mandatory investigation makes people afraid to report harassers. They fear an investigation will become a bigger trauma to them than the original harassment.

☐ "90% of all sexual harassment claims involve individuals who are not aware that their behaviors are offensive or unwelcomed."[6]

☐ We need to consider what is likely to be the work environment after the harassment issue has been settled. How can we help these people to work effectively with each other? Are there places to move harassed people within the company to give them a fresh start?

Guidelines for Employers

The continued modification of civil rights legislation is clearly putting employers at higher and higher risk. So it is crucial that employers enact policies, start employee training and initiate procedures for satisfying any sexual harassment complaints.

Companies need to understand that it's in their best interest to educate people, and the education needs to start with the chairman of the board. "A change in attitudes will follow a mandated change in behavior. Attitudes are not a company's business, but behavior is."[7]

An employer is responsible for acts of sexual harassment in the workplace, whether or not he or she knows about the action. The protection for an employer is to have a policy and procedure in place and to take action on any harassment event.

In an article entitled "Sexual Harassment: A Growing Problem in the Workplace," the author suggests five steps that should be taken by companies to create a harassment-free workplace.

1. Obtain management's full understanding and support.

2. Adopt a formal written policy for dealing with sexual harassment.

3. Widely disseminate the policy.

4. Adopt sanctions for proven cases of sexual harassment.

5. Adopt a formalized complaint procedure.[8]

When the company sets up the sanctions against sexual harassment, it would be helpful to spell out the discipline for each major offense. For example, rape or attempted rape will result in immediate dismissal. Lesser offenses may result in a written reprimand which will be put in the employee's permanent file. Or the employee may be suspended.

Employers should also think through the complaint procedure. Many companies use a chain-of-command structure; an employee who has been sexually harassed is to go to his or her direct superior. But in many cases that person is the sexual harasser. Therefore, companies should set up an independent person to handle sexual harassment complaints.

Specific Suggestions for Management

Steven Anderson, president of his own company and author of *How to Effectively Manage Sexual Harassment,* offers practical insights for employers and managers as they try to eliminate sexual harassment.

Anderson names the top mistakes managers make when conducting sexual harassment investigations:

1. Believing that sexual jokes and banter are a natural part of the workplace culture and that any employee who does not like them is a prude.

2. Trying to resolve complaints personally, without consulting with the organization's appropriate personnel and legal resources prior to dealing with the situation.

3. Deciding that the best way to get rid of the problem is to get rid of the complaining employee.

4. Trying to dissuade the employee from complaining about the sexual harassment (for example, saying to the sexual harassment victim, "Come on, that's just how he is. He was just joking").

5. Acting before the investigation is complete (for example, stating "I'm going to fire the sexual harasser!" before all the facts are in).

6. Making an evaluation of the seriousness of the situation based only on hearsay or partial information or after talking only with the alleged recipient.

7. Not taking it seriously unless it is a formal complaint.

8. Interfering with the sexual harassment investigation of a peer because (a) he/she would never behave like that; (b) it must be a false charge; (c) the alleged recipient is trying to get money from the organization; or (d) the alleged recipient is attempting to ruin the career of the alleged harasser.

9. Not taking the complaint seriously because of assumptions that the alleged recipient asked for the behavior by wearing provocative clothing, flirting, dating several men at the same time, telling sexual jokes and so on.

10. Not taking action when fielding a complaint from an employee in another department. All managers in the organization have a responsibility to the organization and its employees to stop sexual harassment wherever it occurs.

11. Ignoring a complaint because the alleged sexual harassment occurred several years ago.

12. Trying to influence the results of an investigation involving a complaint against top management.

13. Not taking action because the employee who complained of sexual harassment asked his or her supervisor to do nothing.[9]

Each of us must put a stop to harassment. Most women have come to accept the humiliation of harassment as part of their normal working experience. They were forced to put up with it from boys in grade school and later on dates.

How do we work ourselves out of this terrible mess? The next section focuses on helping men understand the awful pain of harassment, as well as giving women the courage to help men understand.

PART TWO

Insights for Men
& for the Women
Who Want
to Help Them

9
Why Men Harass

The bold headline read *Boys Will Be Boys.* Then the story began: "It's hard to be a little girl, going to school every morning with boys who believe in their wormy little hearts that girls stink."

The newspaper continued:

It was particularly hard for seven-year-old Cheltzie Hentz, who had to ride to her school in Eden Prairie, Minnesota, on a bus with boys who called her *bitch,* and a driver who seemed to think it was funny.

"These boys were making fun of the little girls because they didn't have penises!" recalls her horrified mother, Sue Mutziger. Over five months Mutziger sent twenty-two pages of complaints to school officials, who lectured the boys and briefly suspended several troublemakers from riding the bus.

With a new driver this year, the teasing stopped—but Mutziger still thought the schools weren't doing enough to protect her daughter. So she took stronger action: she filed a complaint with the State Department of Human Rights.[1]

Many parents believe that our public elementary schools actually permit the sexual harassment of their daughters. They feel that the boys' verbal jeering, pinching of girls' breasts, flipping up girls' skirts, snapping their bras, and repeated sexual innuendoes in school hallways, parking lots, classes and extracurricular functions are totally out of place and should be stopped.

Parents are beginning to discover that Title IX of the Education Act of 1972 is a powerful weapon against sexual discrimination in the public school systems. Mothers and fathers are filing suit against schools on the same basis that women have been filing harassment suits against employers—for the hostile environment.

And we are seeing only the tip of the iceberg, because many schools are settling out of court. These suits and settlements will not likely change the old "boys will be boys" approach, though, which means "anything goes in the exploitation of girls because that's just the way boys are."

The Spur Posse

The headline declared, "Sex with a Scorecard: A group of high school boys who tallied their conquests ignites a debate over teenage values." The nation was shocked when we heard about the exploits of the Spur Posse. A ninth-grader had met a boy she liked a lot, so she had sex with him. Then he said she had to have sex with his friends too. She didn't want to, but she thought maybe this was the only way to be popular in high school. So she gave in.

In their middle-class Los Angeles suburb of Lakewood, these incidents became known and caused an uproar concerning teenage values. The boys denied charges ranging from sexual molestation to rape. The Spur Posse, a group of twenty to thirty youths, proudly bragged about their competition in which they scored points for each sexual conquest.

The article reported:

Sheriff's deputies arrested eight boys and one young man on more than 17 felony counts of rape, unlawful intercourse and related charges.

Posse members described their exploits with bravado. Founding member Dana Belman, 20, explained that members received a point each time they achieved orgasm with a different girl and boasted that he had scored 63 points. Billy Shehan, 19, bragged that he was the highest scorer, with 66 points. "My parents were a little surprised," he said. "They thought it was more like 50." Shehan said that while many of the boys did not use condoms when intercourse was involved, he did. "I buy them by the boxload," he explained.

Some of the boys' parents seemed unperturbed. At the Belman home, where son Kristopher, 18, had returned after being released from custody, father Donald said, "Nothing my boy did was anything any red-blooded American boy wouldn't do at his age." Billy Shehan's father, Billy Sr., offered a historical perspective. "I'm 40. We used to talk about scoring in my high school," he said. "What's the difference?" Son Billy saw no cause for remorse. "My dad used to brag to his friends. All the dads did."

Diane Hurse, whose son was an original Spur, thought it was "sad for the girls that they have such low self-esteem that they would do this." She found no self-esteem problem in her son's behavior. "What can you do?" she said. "It's a testosterone thing."[2]

For the girls involved, it remains a very big deal. Some of those who complained now endure taunts of "slut." The boys, meanwhile, were cheered when they returned to classes last week. The school is planning several assemblies on date rape and sexual harassment . . . for girls only.

It is important that we not throw up our hands in despair. Boys need to be socialized to respect girls and not see them as playthings. Parents, schools and churches must stop smiling at these actions and view them as serious sexual harassment violations.

"There are still too many people who say 'boys will be boys,' " warns Leslie Wolfe of the Center For Woman Policy Studies in Washington, D.C. "If no one is teaching boys that harassment is wrong, why should they stop harassing women as adults?"

She notes, "Experts also believe that the boy who throws spit balls at girls in his class will grow up to be the man who tries to drop peanuts down their dresses at bars."[3]

Why Do They Do It?

It could be said that there are as many reasons why men harass as men who harass. That might be true, but we need to acknowledge some broad reasons why certain men harass.

Jim and I both have heard stories of mistreatment from women who were wounded by their experiences and yet misunderstood the reasons why they occurred. We want each reader to clearly know that understanding why some men harass *does not justify* harassment or excuse the men who harass. However, understanding some reasons behind harassment will help women know how to deal with harassers. And we hope that as men understand the motivation behind harassment, they will have the courage to change.

Several trends have changed the traditional sex-role definitions, thus causing confusion and resentment. Sometimes these changes have brought men and women into abrasive working relationships. Some of these situations have increased the possibility that women would be harassed.

One trend that has influenced men in recent decades is higher education. Following World War II, our country experienced a great explosion of men and women getting more education. Now men are not the only ones with medical degrees, or who are lawyers, fly airplanes, do plumbing or run road machinery.

Education has changed job stereotypes.

A second trend emerged during World War II when women entered the work force to help the war effort. They took men's jobs so that the men could be freed up for combat. Everyone thought this was temporary. But the women never went back home. They kept working to cover expenses while their husbands went to school on the G.I. bill. Today women are present in the workplace in massive numbers.

A third trend was the civil rights movement that exploded in our country in the sixties. We all became more sensitized to the rights of every human being. Just as it became clear how wrong it is to use derogatory names and attitudes toward an African-American, so now it is clearly wrong to denigrate or sexually harass a woman on the job.

The sixties and seventies delivered another trend: the emergence of the women's movement. Women's liberation was a powerful new force to be reckoned with in every area of society. No longer would women be treated as inferior slaves—they wanted equal power and pay.

Then, the eighties gave expression to the men's movement, which focused on helping men get in touch with themselves, their roots and their fathers.

An Untamed Animal Aggression

All of these movements are clearly positive and should have had a humanizing effect on males. But somehow they missed the mark. Massive numbers of men are tamed by society in some ways, but many men have not experienced much taming of their aggressive biological drives, which often spill over into sexual harassment.

For example, even though society is talking about the "new man," male aggression and violence are on the rise in the U.S. Increasing numbers of women are raped. Gang violence is also rising. Graffiti is everywhere, as young men called "taggers" mark their territories much as a male dog lifts his leg to mark his domain.

In addition, movies and television are increasingly more violent. The movie heroes—James Bond, Arnold Schwartzenegger, Rocky, Bruce Lee, Chuck Norris, Clint Eastwood and John Wayne are the tough-guy idols. Millions of men vicariously live through this kind of model.

Millions of women are also drawn to these strong, violent, macho types. Yet many of these same women experience an ambivalence, saying they want men to be tender, vulnerable, feeling-oriented and exclusively theirs.

Some women have tried to brush off the whole harassment problem as hopelessly impossible to change. Many of these women conclude that men are just animals who think of nothing but sex. "Men," they say, "plan their life and relationships according to the dictates of the little head between their legs."

These counterattacks are not productive. Instead, we need to understand why men harass and what we can do to stop harassment. Yes, certain societal trends have caused some men to harass women, but other, even more basic, reasons need to be considered.

The Male Difference
It's important, at this point, to give a note of balance. The egalitarian movements that started after World War II have led some women to believe that men really are the same as women. We have tended to blur the scientific data that men and women actually are different from the moment of conception.

George Gilder, in a book originally entitled *Sexual Suicide,* quotes extensively from studies, using neuroendocrinological data, which show that "from conception to maturity, men and women are subject to different hormonal influences that shape their bodies, brains, and temperaments in different ways.

"The man is rendered more aggressive, exploratory, volatile, competitive, and dominant, more visual, abstract, and impulsive, more muscular, appetitive, and tall. He is less nurturant, moral, domestic, stable, and peaceful, less auditory, verbal, and sympathetic, less durable, healthy, and dependable, less balanced, and less close to the ground. He is more compulsive sexually and less secure. Within his own sex, he is more inclined to affiliate upwards—toward authority and less inclined to affiliate downward—toward children and toward the weak and needy."[4]

Think about the two different paths boys and girls take from the moment of birth. The baby girl experiences an unbroken line connected to her female sexuality. She is carried in her mother's womb, then in her mother's arms, learns about being a woman from her mother and gradually evolves into being a woman and mother herself.

Can He Make the Double Switch?

The baby boy also experiences the mother's womb, breasts and caressing arms. But, even so, boy babies are not touched and handled by their mothers as much as are girl babies.[5]

Then the boy—being born of a woman and nurtured in the early years by a woman—must make the switch from that nurturing woman to identify with a man, his father. The father likely has not learned to nurture, so the boy surrenders his mother's warmth to follow his father's aloofness.

Sadly, he cannot connect to another woman and her warmth until he proves himself to be a capable man. For centuries, the African Zulu warrior had to kill another man to establish himself as a man. Today, men may prove themselves by attempting a sexual conquest or by harassing women through sexual words and inappropriate touch.

In most cultures of the world, when a young man wants to marry, the woman's parents ask, "How will you provide for our daughter?" They are actually saying, "Show us the evidence that you are successful." He has to prove himself a worthy warrior by society's standards in order to experience again the warmth of a woman's arms and breasts.

Men Continue to Surprise Women

We must emphasize again that simply understanding the biological drives of a man does not excuse men for harassment. We dare not say, "Poor baby! You've had a hard time switching gender models, so it's okay for you to harass."

But we can have hope. All men have aggressive drives; some men have been tamed and socialized. Their aggressive instincts have been directed for people's enrichment and society's betterment, rather than for women's exploitation and men's self-aggrandizement.

Typically, women are puzzled by men's aggressiveness. Women are also bewildered by a man's ability to separate sex from love and commitment. In addition, women are surprised that men are so ill at ease with themselves. "Why do they always try to prove themselves with some sort of conquest, whether in business, professions, athletics or in the sexual arena?" women ask.

To comprehend male harassment, we need to acknowledge male aggressiveness. Women also need to realize that they can be a powerful influence to socialize men.

Because the man has been wanting to reestablish his mother's warmth since early childhood, he may mistakenly attempt to fulfill his need through sexual aggression.[6] If a woman yields to his aggression, the man will not be socialized but reinforced toward more aggression.

The same is true in harassment. The tormenting will not go away unless a woman says, "No!" Women have a powerful influence in taming the harassing male. They must say, "No!" They must report harassment. Men need to realize that warmth and nurturance in a woman is possible only as the male sexual aggressiveness is tamed and replaced by love and commitment.

The Dysfunctional Family History

In *Adult Children of Legal or Emotional Divorce,*[7] we discuss the devastation felt by adults who have been raised in dysfunctional families. We were surprised to discover that people from dysfunctional homes were still struggling with side effects of their parents' turmoil many, many years into adulthood.

In some cases the survey respondents were beyond age forty, with their parents having divorced more than twenty years earlier. Following are the percentages of people who were still struggling with old issues many years later. The statistics are shocking.

☐ 58 percent constantly seek approval
☐ 54 percent lock out some of their past
☐ 53 percent judge themselves too strictly
☐ 51 percent feel they are different from other people because of their parents' conflict and divorce
☐ 50 percent feel stunted in their personal growth
☐ 47 percent take themselves too seriously
☐ 45 percent still were guessing at what is a normal family
☐ 42 percent overreact to situations over which they have no control
☐ 40 percent are still having trouble with relationships
☐ 35 percent have trouble relaxing or having fun
☐ 21 percent have trouble following through on projects[8]

These statistics show an ongoing pattern of dysfunction that gives us some insight into why men might harass women. Of the areas of damage in the lives of adults from dysfunctional homes, two seem to be strongly connected with the man who becomes a sexual harasser: a low self-image and a lack of boundaries.

The Shriveled Self

First of all, he has a low self-image. He frequently covers his damaged sense of self by acting *macho*. If he can make a sexual conquest in even the smallest form—looking up and down a woman's body, brushing against her breasts in the elevator, telling her an off-color joke or that she has shapely legs—he feels some success. These little invasions temporarily prop up his sagging self-image.

Typically, the person with a low self-image also is a perfectionist. He was not adequately loved by his mother and never connected with his father, so he's reaching out for someone to unconditionally love him—to say he's worthwhile.

If the insecure man grasps for love through harassment, he may get a rebuff or, at the least, a tolerant, painful smile from the woman. In either case, it's not what he wanted. So the encounter reinforces his sense of insecurity and worthlessness. Plus, he doesn't understand the reason for his failure or his feelings.

It's important for a woman not to feel that she is responsible for a man's low self-image, or she may allow herself to be sexually harassed, thinking she can help him. Allowing sexual harassment is never right!

A man with a low self-image is afraid to risk a long-term relationship, but still he has this terrific drive to connect to a woman's warmth and caring. Therefore, he uses sexual harassment to give him that surge of adrenaline, without having to commit to the woman. The experience, however, is always a dismal reinforcement of his worthlessness.

The harasser also struggles with the "never enough" syndrome. Because of his inability to connect with women in a significant, long-term way, he resorts to the flash-in-the-pan approach. As he fantasizes over the *Playboy* centerfold or masturbates during a rented X-rated movie, he is led into an abnormal mindset about sexual fulfillment.

Then he stares at the young woman in his office, replaying the fantasies of the distorted movie or pornographic magazine in his mind. He imagines that this live woman with whom he works will respond in the same perverted way the women in the movie or magazine did.

It's easy to see why a man with a poor self-image may try to compensate through harassment. But it only becomes a vicious cycle that drives him farther away from the love he really wants, producing anger and guilt along the way. He needs professional help to break the cycle.

Where Does My Space Stop and Yours Begin?

A second problem area for a man from a dysfunctional home is understanding personal boundaries. In many harassment situations, the man does not know when or where to stop. He doesn't respect other people's space, physically or psychologically.

A man tells a dirty joke to a woman and never asks himself, "Does she want this joke in her psychological space?" The same man may put his arm around his secretary who asks him an innocent question about a project. He does not for a moment pause to ask, "Does this woman want me this close to her physically? Does she like me to touch her?"

His dysfunctional home has not taught him appropriate personal boundaries.[9] He violates others' territory because the lines were confused within his family as he grew up. Of course, he doesn't even know he has a deficiency.

For example, if one parent is an alcoholic, the child is not allowed to continue life as a maturing child within a secure environment. Instead, the parent (sometimes unknowingly) makes demands which force adulthood on the child. The child may have to assume the responsibility for putting the drunk parent to bed, setting the alarm for the next day, and then fixing breakfast for himself, the other children and the alcoholic parent.

When there is marriage dysfunction with parents continually

fighting, children's boundaries are also violated. Parents typically force children to take sides and, in addition, trample on their needs for security, love and physical care.

Or, a man may have been raised in a home with a rigid or domineering mother or father. The parent repeatedly intruded into the child's space by not allowing the child to think for himself, make decisions or have the privilege of success and failure. As a result, that boy steps into adulthood not having experienced boundaries.

In addition, the harassing man likely has had a father who himself was a harasser. Everyone thought it was funny when Dad told crude jokes, touched women inappropriately or constantly put women down. If no one challenges the father or instructs the son, a boy raised in that environment is almost bound to become a harasser.

In fact, this son may even view harassment as one of his rights of passage toward manhood: tell a dirty joke, force a kiss on a girl or touch her breasts in front of the other guys. The ultimate may be to have sex with her and keep her panties as a token. This is much the same as the custom for teenage boys of the Elongot tribe in the northern Philippines who triumphantly bring home the head of a man they have killed to demonstrate their entrance into manhood.

Women vs. Men
The women's movement brought about a necessary correction in our society. Women were not paid equal money for equal work. Women were blocked from promotions because of their gender. In every movement, unfortunately, society changes its thinking only when the protesters overreact and overemphasize their plight and concern.

Suddenly, women were everywhere, demanding equal rights. Many times the demands were not calm requests backed with logical reasoning. Often they were obnoxious, aggressive claims that were deliberately couched in volatile language and emotion to get the attention of the media and thus of the whole population.

Each time a forceful demand is made by a sizable group of people, society shifts to accommodate the new demand. But whenever a societal shift takes place, repercussions and countershifts (sometimes called backlashes) occur.

A Reactionary Movement
We live in Southern California, which is known for earthquakes. For the next several hours, weeks, or months after an earthquake, we experience aftershocks. The earth needs to shift a little bit after an earthquake to settle into a new position. So we experience a lot of tiny aftershocks and a few substantial ones.

Men's response to recent cultural changes has been much like the earthquake aftershocks. The men's movement is reactive, responding to two major cultural forces.

The first force is *the alienation from their fathers*. In 1900, 90 percent of the U.S. population lived in rural areas, mostly on farms. By the year 2000, only a few percent will live in rural areas.

When families moved to the cities, the natural interconnectedness between family members was broken. As a child and teen, I (Sally) grew up sharing field work, caring for animals, gathering eggs, weeding the garden and canning produce and meat. Our family automatically spent time with each other as we worked on our family farm.

If a family moved to the city, the father went off to a job away from home. His children never saw where he worked, let alone shared the work. The hours were long, and bonding between father and son or daughter happened only on the weekend.

The family was further fragmented if the mother went off to work during World War II. In my case (Jim), during the war my father worked twelve hours a day, seven days a week, and my mother worked five days a week. We children had very little parenting. Many days it felt as if we were orphans, taking care of ourselves.

Loss of Power

Today's men's movement seems to be a cry against the disintegration of family relationships, especially between father and son. But it is also a reaction to the women's movement.

As families moved off the farm in the early third of this century, men gained a mysterious power. On the farm the whole family produced the income. Now as city dwellers, the man was providing for his family. A sense of prestige and power is associated with earning the living. No, these men were not out hunting deer or buffalo, but just as surely they came home as victors from the fight, bringing the spoils—a paycheck.

Another force hit when women started to help "bring home the bacon": *men were no longer the sole providers.* The women's rights movement helped women get more nearly equal pay and treatment, but it left men with an uneasy feeling that they had been displaced. Many men were left floundering, and some tried to cover up with renewed chauvinism.

As more women moved into the job market, men painfully realized they were competing not only with men (whom they understood) but also with women (whom they didn't understand). Female traits of sensitivity, intuitiveness and a capacity to connect with people are highly sought after in any people-related business. Women have a natural advantage in conflict management or in sales where the customer must first be treated as a person before he or she will consider the product.

A sizable group of the male population became very angry at women. They felt more comfortable when women were submissive and stayed at home. Men were more secure when women were academically inferior and not as streetwise and workwise as men.

These angry men are likely to seek out the company of other fearful or coarse men who also feel negatively toward women. They reinforce each other's notion that women are out of line. And there is one way they can assert power over those women. Together they laugh and talk about their sexual exploits and brag about their harassment tricks.

These men, who are so irritated and wrathful, often do not realize that their emotions spill over into the nastiness of harassment in a thousand subtle ways. Unconsciously, they try to make life so difficult for a woman that she will leave the job, the dating relationship or the marriage.

Better yet, if they harass with enough power, perhaps that woman will become submissive. This would allow men to vindicate their position of male dominance and verify society's error.

Men must see the cultural changes as permanent and come to value and learn from women as equal partners in all of life. Otherwise, the conflict will continue.

As I write, I (Jim) feel very strongly about this equality. I find that my life is greatly enriched by Sally's insights about life. She is a full partner in our ministry and in the daily life of our marriage. We share the power; we share the responsibilities. We complement each other's weak spots. I wouldn't have it any other way!

10

"Male Pattern Ignorance"

The comic strip shows a prison setting with inmates being prepared for parole through a special class. A goofy penguin is saying to the group, "My name is Opus and I'm a . . . sexual hamster." The female teacher of the group corrects him by saying forcefully, "Harasser!"

Then Opus goes on to reveal his urge to say totally incorrect stuff to women. He explains to the group that it's a result of his "abusive, snoring, nudist parents." He pleads for sympathy as he says, "I'm a victim, victimizing other victims with verbal victimization."

Finally he bangs on the podium and in a crescendo of shouts says, "I'm cured. I'm ready to live a gender-sensitive life." Then he turns to the female trainer of the class and says, "Am I ready for parole, Ma'am?" She responds, "I think you are in good shape."

Opus looks at her body and responds, "Thanks, so's yours."

In the last picture Opus has a chain attached to each arm and leg and is stretched out in a giant "X" upside down on a prison wall.[1]

The Letter of the Law

A lot of harassment training is going on, but are men really changing or are they just being careful? Unfortunately, much of the workers' harassment training is focused not on understanding women or learning to value them as equals, but on what to do or not do to avoid harassment accusations.

To some men the harassment issue is like avoiding a speeding ticket. You get wise about some procedures. You learn that motorcycle policemen typically hide at the bottom of certain hills, and certain towns are known to be speed traps. If you're driving on the freeway, you avoid the left lane since the highway patrol cars typically swoop off the entrance ramps across all lanes to the left one and ticket someone.

The male driver is not saying to himself, "I must drive within the limits." He is saying, "I've got to get a better fuzz buster and watch the mirrors more carefully." *His focus is on avoiding getting caught, not changing his conduct.*

The same attitude is true in the harassment arena. If you're only interested in avoiding being charged with harassment, you have what we are calling "Male Pattern Ignorance." However, if you begin to value and understand women and to see life through their eyes, you won't have a problem with harassment. In addition, you'll find women to be powerful allies and friends for life.

A Woman's Power

Both men and women need to interact with harassment-prevention attitudes. The problem is two-sided. Honest and sincere men are asking, "What do we men do or not do that drives you crazy? What does harassment mean to women? Don't keep telling us we just don't get it. Please, tell us clearly so we *can* get it."

Women need to think definitively about harassment issues, so that when they are asked the question they can give a clearcut explanation. Men work best with concrete ideas, not fuzzy emotions. A woman may say, "You know . . . well, I just feel funny." Or, "I don't know. I just don't like it." That's not enough. You must be more specific. Help the men in your life by thinking clearly ahead of time, so that when the issue comes up you will have specific answers, not just unfocused feelings.

Jim and I are not saying that undefined feelings aren't real. Nor are we saying that harassment isn't real or doesn't cause psychological damage in women. We *are* saying that in order for harassment to be stopped, men and women need to speak clearly in each other's language.

It's fascinating to see how a woman can change a barbarian bachelor into a caring, gentle husband and father. When he is single, he focuses on himself—*his* car, *his* stereo, *his* clothes, *his* money, *his* women, *his* friends. And he uses it all for immediate gratification.

Then he meets the right woman who is strong enough to stand up to him and not play his immediate gratification games. She presses for commitment, marriage, a family, a house to live in, a sacrifice of present gratification for long-term goals for their children and their future.

When a man meets a woman like that, he is changed from a "heathen" to a "husband."

To his bachelor friends he complains loudly. It appears that he has gone into marriage kicking and struggling. But deep within himself he knows this woman is making a good addition to his life. And she is helping him create something that will live beyond himself—his children and his grandchildren.

Without this woman's contribution, he would be caught in an endless whirlpool of immediate gratification and an increasing sense of depression because he doesn't understand how to escape the trap of the self-centered life.

Attitudes That Will Change Male Pattern Ignorance

Following are some suggestions that will help to eliminate harassment:

First, *value each other as equals.* As soon as we use the word *equal,* all kinds of feelings are triggered in men and women. So let's talk about what we mean by *equal.*

Men and women are not the same in many areas. Typically, men are physically stronger; however, women can endure more pain and illness. Men generally have greater physical endurance for such things as running and manual labor, whereas women have quicker reflexes. Often men are good at concepts and gadgetry, while many women have the edge in intuitiveness and understanding human feelings and emotions. So why all this talk that we should value each other as equals?

Equal does not mean *the same.* When we use the word *equal,* we're not saying that men and women can do the same things in the same capacity. Clearly, human experience and scientific investigation have shown that men and women are different. We're using *equal* to mean that both men and women have contributions to make to each other's lives to help us all become whole people. Both are *equally valuable.*

I (Jim) can almost feel some of you guys saying, "Boy, I value my woman—especially if she is pretty and sexy and I can show her off to my friends. And I really value her when we get into bed."

Hear that buzzer blaring? No, that's not a car alarm going off! It's every woman for centuries screaming that you have a very deformed sense of what it means to value a woman.

Only Apples—How Boring!

Now think of the working situation. Women are frequently

devalued because they think differently from men. Often they are not as conceptual. They may not work as well on their own. They like to be in teams and share ideas back and forth. They may not be as committed to the job for vast amounts of overtime or be willing to move to another part of the country. So men say, "It's obvious, women aren't equal to men in a working situation."

Women should not be thought "unequal" if they don't react to business as men do. If we think that way, we've fallen into the trap of comparing apples and apples. We need to see that we are making a fruit salad that will be richer because it has many different flavors. How terribly boring a fruit salad would be if it were only apples. But if we add pineapple, peaches, cherries, melon, guava and papaya, we have a wonderful combination because each fruit makes a special addition.

When businesses are run only by apples, there is just one dimension—a very boring taste. Hey, even Apple Computer realized that it needed to have some variety. It's doing some good stuff with IBM and Sony.

So if you want to stop harassment in your office or in your life, begin to say, "Women are different, but they are equal." In fact, you should appropriately say, "They are *more than equal* to me in lots of areas. I need their contributions in my life to help me be a better person, better employee, better boss, better husband, better father and better lover."

Men everywhere should say out loud, "Women have made a positive, long-term addition to my life."

Second, *learn from women.* One of the most powerful things an organization can do is to set aside time for its people to think creatively about what they are doing, how they are doing it and how it can be done more effectively. A potent way to make the evaluation process more effective is to invite people from outside the organization into the discussions.

People with totally different perspectives bring new insights.

A seafood processing manager might pick up new ideas from people in automobile marketing or fashion design, photography or deep sea diving. The insights of people from different backgrounds may create totally different ways of looking at the way the company functions.

As a result of the collective pool of creative ideas, perhaps the seafood company will change from hauling fish to processing plants on shore to putting processing plants on massive boats, thus producing a higher quality of food.

In the same way, women can make creative contributions to business—or to a man's personal life. Women use language differently. They look at events from a different viewpoint. They have a feeling relationship to people. Many process ideas from an intuitive and idea-sharing approach. They can give a new perspective to the way a situation has been handled, how production should be carried out or what the goals and direction of the organization ought to be.

Unfortunately, many men are not secure and creative enough to allow a woman to teach them. The male ego gets in the way. Many men believe that men are the fountain of all knowledge. If a man hasn't thought of the idea, it must not be a good idea. This arrogant sense of self may also create a problem for some men as they work with other men because they are so unteachable.

If a man is serious about wanting to avoid harassing, he should let women teach him—give him new slants on life and new insights into processes, people and decisions. Then he will be a more well-rounded person. And a man who is learning from women is not the kind who is going to harass a woman. He values her insights too much to exploit her.

Third, *work toward genuine friendships with women.* It might help you to know what kind of men are avoided by women. Here are a few:

Egomaniac: The person who always talks about himself and

who subtly puts you down as he keeps puffing himself up.
Phony: The man who never lets you see his real self. He's always pretending. He keeps changing like a chameleon, depending on which group of people he is with.

Pathetic: The man who whines and complains a lot and tries to get you to be responsible for his problems.

Criticizer: If he is not making "helpful suggestions" to you about yourself or your work, he is criticizing someone else. And you always have the feeling he criticizes you when he talks to others.

Almost everyone wants to avoid these kinds of men, yet many men fall into some of these categories. For example, the macho man who feels that women want to be impressed becomes an egomaniac or a phony, and he doesn't realize that he is driving women—in fact, everyone—away from him.[2]

Now for contrast, let's look at some traits that draw people to other people.

Accepting/Nonjudgmental: Likable people try to understand the views, opinions, ideas and feelings of other people. They don't just focus on their own life. Dr. Paul Tournier, the great and successful French Christian psychiatrist, said that people who came to study his counseling methods were often disappointed, because "I have no methods. All I do is accept people."[3]

Genuine: A part of genuineness is to be "the real thing," just the opposite of phoniness. Likable people are authentic people with integrity. They have pure motives without hidden agendas.

Self-Disclosing: Genuineness refers to being honest in every area of life, whereas self-disclosing people allow others to know them in their successes and failures, their hopes, their dreams, their fears. As they let friends know these things about themselves, their friends, in turn, feel freer to disclose themselves.

Trust: Friendships develop when people can trust that they will not be exploited—whatever is said in confidence will not be used against them.

Caring/Loving: True friends watch the eyes of a friend. When that person's eyes express insecurity, loneliness, self-doubt or fear, a genuine friend moves in to give verbal assurance of the person's worth, perspective on the situation or the simple statement, "I want to help you ride this one out."

Committed: Commitment to a friend is *not* like money you put into a bank, planning to withdraw it someday. Commitment is more like putting oil in your motor. Oil is essential to make the motor operate, but you never plan on taking it out to use again. Its only purpose is to make the motor work effectively.

Enabling: Your friend should be able to say to you, "I'm a better person because of your contributions to my life." Enabling means that you see qualities and abilities in your friend that he or she may not fully recognize. You become the cheerleader, encouraging that person to take the necessary steps to fully utilize all the gifts that God has given him or her.

Spiritually Concerned: Friendships don't move beyond the casual unless they begin to touch the spiritual dimension in each other's lives. Helping a person grow so he or she can handle values, guilt, aspirations, failure and forgiveness is a powerful bond between people.[4]

A man trying to develop strong friendships with women will develop positive traits that promote healthy, mutual relationships. This growth in his personality will also lift him out of the "Male Pattern Ignorance" of harassment.

But what about the men's movement? Will all that beating of chests and drums out in the woods help with the harassment issue? Read on as we tackle that issue.

11

What Men
Don't Know
Will Hurt Them

S ome basic facts related to the sexual harassment issue can help you—or kill you if you ignore them. Walk with us through these areas so that you're not caught off guard.

In the movie "My Fair Lady," Professor Higgins is frustrated as he tries to understand and tutor a young woman. Finally, to a friend he blurts out, "Why can't a woman be like a man?"

Men know women look different from men, but most are unaware that women think, feel and process life very differently than they do. Many men are even more blind to how sexual harassment affects women.

Men's ignorance about harassment issues stems partly from not understanding that it is not really about sex—it's about power. Men use their power to take advantage of women.

What's even more insidious is that most men don't see that they have a power advantage, thus adding indifference to injury. They mistakenly think that if women didn't like it, they would say something. They can't understand how frightened a woman is to try to stop a powerful man or even to speak against him to another person.

On April 2, 1992, at the invitation of Yale Law School Dean Guido Calabresi, Anita Hill returned for the first time to her alma mater to deliver the 1992 Dean's Lecture. She received three standing ovations from the overflow crowd of students and faculty, with Calabresi honoring her as a symbol for her time, an individual who "stood up as few can ever hope to do." The following are excerpts from her address:

> Legalized slavery [has] ended in the United States, but unfortunately, documented sources explain that sexual harassment and abuse of the country's farm workers, factory workers, office workers and domestic workers has endured.
>
> While the relationship of ownership and power involved in slavery do not exist in the university or the workplace today, relationships of power are a part of the academic and work environments. Faculty and administrators have power over students, supervisors over employees, and often senior employees in non-supervisory positions have power over other employees. Unfortunately, abuse of power exists in those relationships as well.
>
> Because the power relationships are not as extreme in modern times as in slavery, we can expect that most of the abuses suffered at the present are not as extreme as the abuses suffered in slavery. Nevertheless, many of the abuses suffered are repugnant to our sense of decency, and many, many more are in violation of the legal standards established under federal law.[1]

It's crucial that women speak out, telling the men in their lives that sexual harassment is an improper use of power. Men need to know they aren't making matters better by saying, "That's the way life is, just put up with it."

Here are several things men must do:

First, *understand the power issue from a woman's point of view.*

Men need to put themselves in the shoes of harassed women. Frequently, men themselves are harassed in job situations, so if a man can acknowledge and feel his own harassment, he will gain a great deal of sensitivity toward sexually harassed women.

Think of Bruce, a young lawyer who joins a firm at a $30,000 salary and is promised that, if he does well, he'll get a sizable raise at the end of the year. Because he lives in Southern California and housing expenses are extremely high, he needs to be earning about $40,000 to make ends meet. Because he doesn't earn that much, his wife, Shirley, must go to work, and they both are caught in the harassing snare: "If you do well, you'll get a sizable raise."

None of the terms are spelled out. What does "doing well" mean and what is a sizable raise? Now Bruce is an easy victim. He is given extra assignments, research and depositions. In short, he takes on almost any job that anybody wants to get rid of so that he'll come across to his superiors as "doing well." Bruce is in the office early in the morning, stays late at night, takes work home over the weekend and cuts short his family vacations so he can be in court for a crucial case. His work week easily escalates to 100 hours.

What does Bruce do about it? He doesn't like taking time away from his young family. He wants to be with his wife. He's missing out on the two kids and their special little moments. But he doesn't dare tell his boss this. He's afraid to rock the boat. He keeps thinking, dreaming, hoping it will get better.

At the end of the first year, during his first annual review, they smilingly pat him on the back. "Bruce, you've done a terrific job. We're so proud of you. You're the kind of person we're looking for to be part of our team long-term. Somewhere down the road we even want to make you an associate partner in this firm."

The Carrot

Now the bait is out there again. There's no definition of when he'll get a promotion or raise, or what he must do to earn it. Nothing is spelled out. Rather, the hidden meaning is, "Just work like crazy and we'll reward you however we think fitting."

At the end of the review, in a rather dramatic gesture, the boss says, "We're giving you a raise, Bruce, and a bonus. This next year your salary is going to be $31,000. Plus, we are giving you an additional $500 bonus. You've done a good job and we're looking forward to bigger salary raises and bonuses in the future, not to mention that associate position."

What does the young man say? "This is really puny! I was looking for at least a $5,000 raise. Come on, guys! Get real with the cost of living in this area."

Dare he say that to these powerful people who can make or break his career? He probably won't say a word unless he is terribly gutsy and has some other alternatives. He may start looking for another job, but the lure of becoming a law firm associate at his young age is a very powerful enticement to stay.

The true story at this writing is that this young man has worked for the firm for four years. Each year he has received only a very small cost of living increase. He has been assured again and again that he will become a partner in the firm, but nothing has materialized other than broad smiles, slaps on the back and endless promises.

If a man can put himself into Bruce's shoes or remember his own ugly experiences of being harassed at a job, he's in a position to click into an understanding of the power issues for women. Perhaps he can begin to empathize with a woman's feelings of shame, guilt and diminished self-worth when she is sexually harassed.

Second, *remember that men often oversexualize what women say and do.*

If a woman at the office says, "John, I like your new suit,"

John thinks, *She wants my body. She wants to go to bed with me.* If John sees the same woman walking toward him in the hallway and she smiles, he says to himself, *She wants me.*

Because men are prone to sexualize almost everything a woman says or does, a man with a sexual harassment tendency will think the woman wants him to give her sexual attention. He feels justified in touching, hugging, patting her or telling suggestive stories. *After all, didn't she smile at me in the hallway and didn't she tell me my new suit looks great? She wants my touching and my remarks.*

When you are beginning to feel that a women is sexually attracted to you, cut your evaluation in half—it will probably be more realistic.

Third, *ask hard questions about the men's movement.*

Men meeting with men is not enough. I (Jim) wonder if the men's movement led by Robert Bly *(Iron John)* may be leading men to a new, repressive attitude toward women. Men are out in the woods, beating their chests and drums, trying to connect to their feelings and to their fathers. And these activities can be an important step toward recovery. But men meeting *only* with men do not become fully humanized.

A subtle macho image is reinforced as men get down in the dirt on all fours, facing each other and putting their shoulders against each other while they try to drive each other backwards. It all looks like a game, but there's a reinforcement of competition and individual assertiveness that must be channeled or it will create greater problems between the sexes.

Separation from women will not make a man fully male. Yet this is a strong concept taught in some parts of the men's movement. Certain African tribes are held up as the model. In those tribes, young boys live with their mothers until puberty. Then the men of the community, who live in separate huts from the women, come to the women's huts where these young boys live and call them out. They are taken away and taught how to be men. They will never again return to women other than for procreation.

The extremists in the men's movement seem to be saying, "If you really want to be a man, you'll abandon all this woman stuff and come running in our male herd."

In order for young men to be whole people, boys need to be taught by their fathers *and* their mothers what it means to be a man. The young boy can then develop qualities that are typically found in males—strength, courage, aggressiveness—and qualities found in females—sensitivity, tenderness, intuitiveness.

Creation teaches the value of both men and women. Our culture at this time is unsettled about male and female roles and wrestles with the gigantic harassment issue. We desperately need to clearly hear what happened at Creation. After God had created the world as we know it and filled it with flowers and trees, birds, animals, fish and other living creatures, he then created man.

For each of his previous acts of creation, God declared that *it was good.* However, in Genesis 2:18, after the creation of man, God says, "*It isn't good* for man to be alone; I will make a companion for him, a helper suited to his needs."

The clear statement here was that man was not complete in himself. He needed something more. There were emotional gaps in his personality that could *only* be met by another person.

Notice that God did not create another *man.* He didn't establish a "herd" or "pack" of men; his choice was a *woman.* And then God declared his work to be *very good.*[2] But she too was an incomplete being and needed the companionship of the man. They needed each other in order to be fully human.

History has shown again and again that whenever men begin to run in packs, they tend to be barbarians. This is true whether they run in packs on Wall Street, as surfers on Southern California beaches, in the gangs of our major cities or as drug lords ruling the cocaine traffic and millions of people's minds. Whenever men are isolated in the company of men, they tend to become less than human. Men need women to be saved from the hell of their own making.

Fourth, *shake off the male myths about sexual harassment.* What men don't know about women becomes obvious when we look at what some men believe about harassment:

Myth: Sexual harassment affects only a few women.

Fact: Several surveys have documented the widespread nature of sexual harassment. In one study, 88 percent of the respondents said they had experienced one or more forms of unwanted sexual advances on the job.

Myth: Sexual harassment is rare on campuses.

Fact: Women have only recently begun to talk about the long-hidden problem of sexual harassment among students, staff and faculty. Fear of ridicule, a sense of hopelessness about the problem and a feeling that it's a "personal" dilemma have kept the issue concealed.

Myth: Women should ignore sexual harassment when it occurs.

Fact: In one survey, 33 percent of those reporting sexual harassment at work had at first tried to ignore the unwanted attention. In 75 percent of these, the harassment continued or became worse. One-quarter of the women who ignored the sexual propositions received unwarranted reprimands from their bosses or had their workloads increased.

Myth: If a woman really wants to discourage unwanted sexual attention, she can do so. If she's sexually harassed, she must have asked for it.

Fact: Many men believe a woman's no is really yes, and so they do not accept her refusal. Additionally, when a man is in a position of power, such as employer or teacher, the woman may be coerced or feel forced to submit.

Myth: Most charges of sexual harassment are false. Women

use these charges as a way of "getting back" at a man with whom they are angry.

Fact: Women who openly charge harassment risk not being believed, being ridiculed, losing their job, receiving a bad grade or being mistreated in some other way. Women have little to gain from false charges.

Myth: Sexual harassment is not harassment at all. It is a purely personal matter between men and women. It's a fact of life.

Fact: When a woman is coerced by a professor or her employer, she is not always in a position to readily reject such overtures, or if she does, she may face adverse reactions. Several courts have ruled that sexual harassment on the job constitutes sex discrimination under Title VII of the Civil Rights Act, and in some instances have awarded damages to women.[3]

"Okay, okay," you may be thinking, "I'm beginning to understand that I *don't* understand all I need to know about preventing harassment! But how can I change?" The next few chapters will help you with practical guidance for your daily life.

12
What Men Need to Know About Women

Leroy is an obnoxious pest. He continually harasses the women in the small manufacturing plant where he works. About 75 percent of the employees are women, and most of them view Leroy as disgusting yet harmless.

Leroy's style is what we're calling *low-level harassment*. It's probably not the kind that would cause the average woman to file a complaint, but his attitude and behavior are aggravating.

Leroy is a sad case—*he doesn't even know what he doesn't know about women*. He thinks women like what he does. He believes he and the women are good friends. He doesn't realize that they don't want to be his friend. None of them would ever, *ever* consider dating him if he were single. They just put up with him the same way we all put up with a dripping faucet—probably we should fix it, but it's not *that* bad.

Leroy's harassment takes three forms. First is his disgusting use of words. He never refers to any of the women by name. It's always "Honey," "Babe," "Hi, Sexy," and "Hey, Beautiful."

Leroy doesn't understand that women find it demeaning to be called by a physical feature rather than by their name.

Leroy's second annoying harassment is *touching.* He looks for opportunities to give women a quick hug, to pat their arms or, if they're seated, to pat them on the knee. One of his most annoying habits is to poke his finger through any opening in a woman's blouse or dress where skin shows. He's careful not to poke in front—that would be going too far. But Leroy doesn't know that women don't like to be poked, except affectionately by their husband or lover.

Third, Leroy likes to tell *off-color stories and jokes.* When the women respond with an embarrassed, half-hearted laugh, he thinks they like his stories—and him. He doesn't get it. Leroy is a nuisance and he doesn't realize that women can't stand him. As we said, Leroy *doesn't know what he doesn't know about women.*

A female employee was asked, "How do you feel about what Leroy does and says?" She responded, "He just comes with the job. I don't pay any attention to him. He's harmless." When we asked further, "But would you want to be his friend?" she responded, "No way, José! In fact, I feel sorry for his wife. He doesn't have the first clue about relating to a woman."

Leroy is trapped back in the free-love thinking of the sixties and seventies. The sexual revolution shaped his perception of women. He saw women to be more like men because they went off to work. He also believed women, like men, would take love or sex where they could get it. He assumed that women too were sexually aggressive and always "on the make."

It's true that the women's movement pushed many women beyond where they felt comfortable. Many burned their bras, disdained marriage and sold themselves 100 percent into career and casual relationships. But during the eighties and nineties, women returned to more balanced lives.

Women now want more romance, candlelight, music, gifts, dinners, courting and complimenting. No, they don't want to give up the gains they made by being independent women, but neither do they want to give up the satisfying relationships of marriage, family and lifelong commitment.

The tragedy is that Leroy is stuck. He doesn't even know that women have changed. He thinks of himself as a rooster in a henhouse where all the hens want to be inseminated.

Leroy Believes He's a Stud

Previously, we've said that sexual harassment is not only about sex but also about power. That's true, but almost always a dimension of raw sex is attached to the harassment. In Leroy's situation, he would be glad to have sex with several of the women where he works. Because none of the women respond and because Leroy is not obnoxiously aggressive, nothing will ever happen. Nevertheless, sex is always obsessively on Leroy's mind.

However, Leroy doesn't know how little he knows about a woman sexually. Not only is he a failure in carrying out his macho sexual images at work, but he's also failing his wife because he doesn't understand women. Of course, Leroy blames his inadequate, perfunctory marital sex life on his wife: "I just didn't marry the right kind of woman."

When he says "the right kind of woman," he thinks his wife is odd and every other woman is like the paid sexual performers in magazines or video movies. Leroy doesn't even understand that those women are paid to respond to men's fantasies. They are not real women.

If a man wants to escape thinking and acting like pathetic Leroy, he must become friends with a woman instead of only using her sexually. To escape the Leroy syndrome, he needs to know and act on some basic information.

What Men Need to Know

First, *study the life agenda of your wife or female friend.* A woman is strongly drawn to a man who understands her stage in life and is not just trying to get her "into the sack." For example, a woman in her early twenties is deciding what abilities God has given her. She's trying to get started in the world of education and/or a career. She may also be considering marriage and a family.

By the late twenties or early thirties, women experience a reassessment time when they ask, "How am I doing? Am I accomplishing the things I thought I would accomplish when I was twenty-two? What should I change? What are the risks involved in changing?"

By her late thirties, a woman is experiencing a mid-life transition which may become a mid-life crisis. She may be wrestling with issues of aging, teenage children, a dissatisfying marriage, career frustration—a general sense that life isn't turning out to be what she expected. This can be an extremely frustrating time. A man who understands her can become her ally. Our book *Women in Mid-Life Crisis* will help you to understand a woman at this age.[1]

By the late forties or early fifties, a woman will experience menopause, minor signs of aging, the realization that retirement (previously something only for "the older generation") will affect *her* in a few years. And all of this is possibly combined with the empty nest and grandmothering. She goes through a great number of physical changes, and her emotions may be skyrocketing or crashing. The instability causes her pain and affects everyone around her as well.

Many women experience some of these emotional dips in their late thirties or early forties. Sometimes they're regarded as PMS (premenstrual stress syndrome), but studies show that sometimes they are actually premenopausal symptoms.[2]

If you as a man understand what's likely to happen in the various stages of a woman's life, you'll be in a position to become her friend. Unfortunately, many men don't focus on learning about women in general or even about their wife; they just assume she's going to be the same for the rest of her life.

Knowing the woman's life agenda will help a husband or lover to become a best friend. He's not trying to exploit her but be supportive, give counsel and provide insight. He wants the very best for her.

Second, if you want to be a woman's friend, *understand what she likes in a man.* Almost every women's magazine reports periodically on what women are looking for in men. Some surprising traits keep showing up in these summaries of reader surveys about what women find appealing in men.

A mind is one trait that women are drawn to in a man. An intelligent, insightful and thoughtful man who is also witty is very attractive to women.

Confidence is a second trait mentioned in these surveys. Women are attracted to a man who understands himself and people, and who then uses that knowledge to confidently accomplish things in his own life, as well as helping others accomplish their goals.

Voice is another quality women notice. If a man has a soft, rather deep voice, and if he uses that voice to communicate care as well as wisdom, women are powerfully attracted.

A man who *genuinely likes women* as people possesses another trait women appreciate. This kind of man can interact with a woman as another interesting and intelligent human, instead of always seeing her sexuality as the primary thing. He will have no trouble finding women friends.

True understanding and friendship become the powerful forces that draw a woman to a man, whether in a dating relationship, marriage or some educational or work setting.

"But I've Got a Great Body"

Men ask, "Aren't women interested in my body?" Yes, they are. But think for a moment about how differently men and women are first attracted. A man starts by looking at a woman's body. If she passes all his tests, he then begins to find interest in other dimensions of her personality. But he never loses that strong focus on her body.

Yes, women are interested in a man's body, but it might surprise you what part of a man's body is most attractive to them. In a recent *Esquire* poll, eyes ranked as the sexiest part of a man's body; buns took second place. In most polls, hands ranked third. One woman said, "The first thing I look at is his eyes. One look in a man's eyes and I know right away if I'm interested."[3]

Many women, attracted by a man's eyes, believe they can read his character by his eyes. A woman doctor from Pittsburgh put it this way, "It's all in the eye contact. If his eyes dart around and avoid you nervously, that's a sure sign he's not very self-confident. A man who can't sustain eye contact with a woman is a washout—with me, at least."[4]

Isn't it strange that men are spending a lot of time getting their bodies in shape, when they ought to be working on the inner self which is seen in the eyes? A man must become a whole person who honestly understands himself and sincerely uses his God-given abilities to help other people become all they can become.

While you should be working on your inner man, this certainly doesn't mean you shouldn't keep your body in good shape—they *are* looking at your buns. But if you think the average woman is going to be attracted because you are muscle-bound, you're dead wrong. In fact, too many muscles turn a lot of women off. Keep yourself physically fit, but also pay attention to good personal hygiene. Brush your teeth, keep your hair neat and wear clothes that are neither high-fashion nor super-grubby.

The ABCs of Bonding
If you genuinely want to connect with a woman, you need to understand *how* to be her friend. Here are some guidelines:

First, *listen to her.* This serves two purposes: to understand her and to release her tension. Realize where she is in her life's stages and the kinds of issues she's dealing with. She needs empathy. Talking gives her an opportunity to ventilate and release her built-up tension.

Listening is not a passive process. Try to draw her out. As she talks about her struggles, ask her, "How does that make you feel?"

Listening is not for the purpose of solving problems. It's to draw out emotions. It's better to ask only questions that help her to talk more. Don't suggest solutions. Give her the opportunity for anxieties to drain off.

Second, *express the feeling side of yourself.* When you talk about your job, share how you feel about it, not just what you think. If you're discussing the children, a hobby, your future or buying a car or new clothes—tell her how you feel. You are more likely to develop a deep bond with a woman as you communicate on a feeling level.

Third, *encourage her to change and to grow.* If she expresses anxiety about her job, feeling as if she's not going anyplace, tell her that you stand behind her. Let her know that she's got a lot more to offer to the world than what this job is allowing. Tell her she doesn't need to put up with the degrading experiences she is going through.

Perhaps she needs to be encouraged to go back to school. Maybe she's afraid she won't be able to keep up. If you are her husband, she may ask, "How can we afford it?" or "Who will do the other work?" Help her to see that you really want her to grow and that you'll do all you can to facilitate that.

Maybe she needs an adventure, a new experience. Has she talked about painting, wanting to scuba dive, taking more mini-breaks from her work, traveling? Encourage the adventurous part of her life.

If you do these things, she'll begin to look at you as her best friend. She'll feel you're someone who wants to help her attain everything that's possible for her life.

Fourth, *affirm her.* Affirmation takes many forms. Typically, we think of affirmation as *words,* and words are very important. When you speak words of affirmation, look directly into her face and compliment her about a specific item.

Focus on the qualities of her life, not simply on her activities or the things she does for you. Qualities, such as caring for people or being generous, are attributes that continue for all of life. A time may come when she won't be physically able to go scuba diving. It's okay to affirm that ability now, but accept the possibility that it won't last all her life. Yet she can always be a caring, generous person.

Another way to affirm is by warm *touching.* A hug, a pat on the shoulder or a good backrub will help your wife or girlfriend know that you really do care for her. Learn the way the special woman in your life likes to be touched in nonsexual ways. Touching without sex in mind is very affirming to women.

Giving *little gifts* will also help her to know that you think she's special. It can be as simple as a card, a surprise plant, a single rose or a little memento that you bring back from a trip. She likes to know that you've been thinking about her and you picked out something especially for her.

Sometimes it's helpful to *affirm at the very point of anxiety.* For example, as the two of us are getting older, we're developing wrinkles on our faces. Sally tells me that wrinkles give my face a mature warmth. And Jim tells me those crows' feet around my eyes are really smile lines that make my eyes look warm and friendly. It feels good to sense acceptance about something that really bothers us.

Take courage. You can get far beyond poor old Leroy. You can learn to succeed in relationships with women—both those you interact with casually and that special woman who will enrich you for a lifetime.

13
To Do and Not to Do

Roy is sixty-two years old. He's a warmhearted, likable person who manages a branch office for a temporary employment agency. His response regarding the harassment issue is probably typical of most men over fifty: "It's a lot of fuss about nothing. Nobody means anything by it when they call a woman *honey*. I certainly don't think of myself as harassing if I compliment a woman on the clothes she's wearing." Then Roy paused, looked around the room and said, "But it's a new ball game now. I certainly don't want to get nailed with a harassment charge, so I address everyone by their first name.

"I'm trying to be very careful," Roy continued. "I don't comment about how a woman looks or the clothes she's wearing. I don't ask about her personal life or her family, even if I see a picture on her desk. I don't say anything. Maybe I'm overreacting. But I am the branch manager, and I sure don't want any lawsuits. One thing I can tell you, though. The whole harassment thing has made everybody almost afraid to talk to each other. It's just not as much fun coming to work as it used to be."

Different men deal differently with the harassment issue. One kind of man absolutely believes that women have been harassed and it's about time our society responded to their legitimate concerns. These men want training programs and prevention procedures to stop harassment.

A second group, often men with little or no power in organizations, feels that the harassment accusations are way out of line. These men think they have a right to do what they want to do. Period. They believe women want "real men." In their thinking, that means men who chase women, talk sexy and give them a little pat on their posterior. They believe women secretly want to be chased and patted. To them, this whole harassment thing is just baloney. They see harassment as weeding out the "men" from the "boys."

A Bunch of Foolishness
Some people you know may feel that the debate on sexual harassment has gone too far and is just a bunch of foolishness. In an editorial entitled, "We Don't Need This Nonsense," the writer, commenting on the continued refining of the definition of harassment, says, "In other words, it is now illegal to cause someone embarrassment in the work place. It is illegal to be insensitive. It is illegal to be impolite.

"What other unspeakable acts will we be protected from? Well, leering, for one. Yes, Orwell's worst nightmares have come true. Rulers are now attempting to control by law the expressions people may have on their faces.

"What else? The display of sexually offensive material is also forbidden. The cover of *MacLean's* magazine for March 9, 1992, in order to publicize its feature article on breast implants, showed a young woman nude from the waist up, with arms crossed over her clearly ample breasts. What if someone on my staff found this embarrassing? Should I have banished *MacLean's* from my reception area? Should I have torn off the cover?

"Whatever happened to that ancient legal maxim, *de minims non curat lex* (the law does not concern itself with trifles)? Wouldn't it be better if those who are embarrassed by non-gross, non-vulgar sexist jokes, leers or pictures simply took an assertiveness course and polished up a few incisive put-downs and withering glares of their own?"

The author continues, "The most vicious part of the sexual harassment witch hunt is the case law holding employers vicariously liable for acts of sexual harassment among their employees, if they fail to take steps to prevent or rectify it.

"But what steps are enough? Does an employer have to expose himself to a wrongful dismissal lawsuit by the alleged harasser in order to avert a sexual harassment lawsuit by the alleged victim? What could be more patronizing that this entire policy? How better to undermine the professional image of working women than to make our male colleagues believe that we need or want this fascist nonsense to protect us from them?"[1]

To victims of harassment, however, it doesn't seem like nonsense to change the environment that degrades and embarrasses them. They identify with the dictionary definitions of *harass:* To disturb or irritate persistently; to wear out, exhaust; to enervate by repeated raids; to hound (relentlessly pursue); to badger, pester, plague, bait, or torment.[2]

A third group consists of men who, like Roy, are confused and want direction. They have realized there is a problem but are unsure how to respond.

These men truly don't want to offend women. But they also don't realize how conditioned they are toward harassing women.

Many of these men grew up in homes where the mother was treated with little or no respect, where the father demanded sex as part of the mother's bargain in marriage, where there was the flagrant violence of verbal or physical abuse.

Men from these homes may be carrying a very exploitative

view of women that allows them to repeatedly cross over the sexual harassment barrier and not even realize it.

Things Are Changing

In the late eighties a transition gradually started in how courts and juries viewed harassment. When a harassment charge was brought into court before the late eighties, the decision would be made on the basis of what a "reasonable man" would think of the working environment.

In a number of cases from 1986 to 1989, the defense clearly conceded that there was offensive conduct including words, gestures, touching, explicit posters and crude and suggestive language. Yet these cases were all lost because the basis of deciding the case was on what a "reasonable man" in that work environment would think about these items or behaviors.

During this period, U.S. Circuit Judge Damon J. Keith filed a dissenting opinion in which he said that the test of harassment ought not to be what the "reasonable man" thought but, rather, what a "reasonable woman" would think in this situation. His opinion was overruled—but nevertheless it was in the record.

In 1991, a case known as Ellison vs. Brady became a watershed for the test of conduct and of whether a hostile environment existed. The judgment was made on the basis of the "reasonable woman," not the "reasonable man."

Since the Ellison case was won on the grounds of what a "reasonable woman" would think, many cases have been won using that same approach. Our legal system will no longer allow the harasser or his peer group to decide what is reasonable behavior.[3]

The "Don't Do" List

Now let's get very specific about what not to do. Remember, these coaching comments are intended not to save you from lawsuits but to help you learn correct ways to relate to women.

Don't touch. Limit your touching to your wife or your girl-friend. Indiscriminate patting and hugging are considered a violation and are definitely on the "Don't Do" list. In addition, almost every woman views pinching, patting her bottom or touching her breasts as a chargeable harassment offense. Lawsuits are being won over this type of touching. Touch can be one of those gray areas, but it's better to touch only in commonly acceptable ways, such as shaking hands.

Don't talk inappropriately. Suggestive sexual talk such as dirty jokes, discussing sex scenes from movies or describing your personal sex life will be viewed by many women as a violation of their psychological space. If you go further and tell a woman how good her legs look or how well she fills out her sweater, or even as far as to say you'd like to have sex with her, you're certainly establishing grounds for a winnable sexual harassment suit against you.

In addition, if you even hint that she might get a promotion, a raise or some other perk or favor by being willing to have sex with you, you're in what we call "deep yogurt"! Your situation is a lawsuit waiting to happen.

Remember, if she files a report with an official in your company, two things are likely to occur. One, depending on the severity of the case, you may be suspended or lose your job, and two, her attorney will press for a financial claim against the company. And most assuredly, she will also file a claim against you.

You likely will be crippled in your employability and earning power for the rest of your life. So suggestive language is also on the "Don't Do" list and is serious stuff.

Be careful with your eyes. There's a difference between glancing at a woman and staring or ogling. A glance is just that. It's done in a millisecond. It's a moment of recognition that the other person exists—but it is no more than that.

A common rule of thumb applies in interpersonal relationships when people meet. If the person looks at you for more than half a second, he or she is expressing an interest in you. If your acquaintance looks at you for as much as two or three seconds, he or she is definitely attracted to you. That's important information to know if you are dating. But if you look at women in the office, the elevator or at the office party for more than a second, you're starting to walk on thin ice. If a woman a couple of desks away notices you repeatedly looking at her for more than one second, she's going to get uneasy. It may irritate her enough to file a report against you.

So you are asking, "What if I want to date someone? I am attracted. I want to look at her. I want to communicate to her that I am interested."

Then it's best not to just stare at the person from a distance. It's better to move close, look squarely in her eyes, and say, "I notice that we take coffee breaks at the same time. I wonder if I could join you sometime."

Now your looking at her is appropriate. She expects to be looked at when she is being talked to. It's the looking *without* verbal communication that will get you in trouble.

Some ways of looking at a woman who is not your wife are always on the "Don't Do" list. If you look up and down her body, you are in potential trouble. If you stare at her breasts or you take a step back and look at her legs, you are definitely harassing! If this is a repeated pattern with the same woman, she's going to consider it harassment and she will likely file a complaint.

Don't misuse your power. You have more power if you are her boss or supervisor, have been with the company longer, earn more money, have a higher title or more education. Just being male gives unspoken power.

It's crucial that any evaluations or discussions of promotions or raises not be based at all on a woman's attractiveness to you.

These decisions should be based only on the company's needs and the work record and capabilities of the people being considered. If you've previously not been sensitized to the whole harassment issue, you must become aware that your power position makes you vulnerable. Your use of power over a woman should also be added to the "Don't Do" list. Your position is vastly different from that of the teenage boy who works on the loading dock part-time. You have more to offer to a less powerful woman in your company; you also have far more to lose than that teenage boy.

Misuse of Power at Home

Power is also an issue in many marriages. Men who might be careful not to abuse power at work may do so at home. If you view your mate as your servant, or as someone who owes the family a certain amount of money from her job plus household upkeep, childcare and regular sex for you—you are abusing your power in the marriage relationship.

Couples in strong marriages have a deep commitment to each other. But that commitment is *voluntary*. Each mate *chooses* to serve and satisfy the other rather than being pressured only by marriage vows or legal status. If you need help to enrich your marriage, you might enjoy reading *Traits of a Lasting Marriage*.[4]

Dating Protocol

"What about dating people from work?" you ask. There are many different viewpoints. Some men are saying, "I won't date anyone from work—I'm afraid." They aren't afraid of the actual dating process but of a sexual harassment charge as they go through the stages of asking for a date.

Our counsel about dating someone from work is midway between the two extremes of never dating and pretending the harassment issue is not real. If you're interested in someone, think through all we've said about what men need to know about women. Focus on being the right kind of person—friendly, supportive, encouraging. In other words, build a friendship.

In the friendship-building process, you may begin to get signals that the woman appreciates you and values your friendship. These signals do not automatically mean that she wants to date you; she may only enjoy your friendship. So continue to go slowly.

After some weeks or months of friendship-building, suggest that you have lunch together. At lunch use all the skills for deepening your friendship that we referred to in a previous chapter. These skills are also discussed in very practical detail in *Making Real Friends in a Phony World*.[5]

After the successful lunch, wait a couple of weeks. Then ask her if she would like to go out for dinner. Now you are on your way into a normal dating relationship that may either succeed or fail. But, at least, you're not likely to be charged with harassment if you take this go-slow approach.

Word of Caution

However, one situation is an absolute no-no. Don't date someone in your company with lesser power than yours. Never date a client if you are a counselor or a medical doctor.

If you are interested in someone less powerful at work and you feel you *must* seriously consider dating her, perhaps you or the woman could transfer to another department so there are no power issues involved. If you're in a professional relationship where she is your patient or client, refer her to someone else. Only after you've clearly had no professional relationship for a period of time should you consider approaching her for a friendship or dating relationship. (Some state laws require counselors to leave a two-year gap of time before dating, while other states totally prohibit contact.)

The "To Do" List

Much antiharassment training focuses on how to avoid being sued on harassment charges. While it's important to be defensive, remember that football games aren't won by teams who are *only* great defensive teams. You have to put some points on the board. You must take the offensive—start moving the ball. You must be aggressive.

The same thing is true in a relationship with a woman. It's not enough just to be careful that you're not doing the wrong thing. Then you live in fear all the time. It's better to be on the offensive. Let your male aggressiveness come into play here. Start doing *positive* things that will not only move you away from the possibility of harassment charges but also make you a better liked coworker, husband and friend.

Praise. You'll never be charged with harassment if you compliment a woman for the excellent work she's done. You can also praise her for her positive, upbeat attitudes around the office, as well as her qualities of helpfulness. Give her specific illustrations: "Thank you for jumping in with extra effort and time to get that last project out. It was crucial to all of us and the boss was really pleased. You made us all look good."

Respect. Use respectful words, not sexual putdowns, such as, "This meeting is for men only—you girls wouldn't understand these problems in our company." (Notice that women do not want to be called girls, a term which implies less stature and even childishness.) Think of the women you work with as part of a team. Listen to their ideas and incorporate those ideas into an information base for decision-making.

The harassment issue has tended to focus everyone toward work accomplishments. That narrow focus may cause us to ultimately lose respect for people as we begin to see them as simply producers—machines without feelings. Inquire specifically for a person's opinion. Ask, "How could things be done better?" It will help your fellow employees feel they are respected and valued as persons by you.

Equality. We aren't trying to make everyone think alike or all have the same abilities. It's important to value the differences in people as each makes an important contribution to the whole effort. Equality, then, is seeing each person's importance and rewarding that value through verbal affirmation in private or in front of the group. An advancement in position or an increase in salary also shows they are worthy and equal.

Fair treatment. Help your people—women and men—improve their skills and advance in their jobs. Give them opportunities to take on new responsibilities, to work with more advanced equipment and to focus their energies in the areas where they feel most gifted.

An easy way to help change the potentially harassing atmosphere in an office is to promote more women to higher positions. That causes an automatic change in the atmosphere. These promotions show that women are being valued.

Not all changes have to be permanent. Make a woman chairperson of a committee. Put her in charge of gathering data for a planning meeting. Ask her to "brief" others who will be part of a future meeting. Even temporary assignments are important transfers of power. Worth and value are communicated to the specific woman, to other female workers in the office and to the men. Then, when she is promoted to vice president, everyone will respect her in the new position.

A few years ago I (Jim) was the director of a doctoral program at Biola University in California. The program was rather new and had previously had only part-time leadership. Since the program was expected to grow rapidly, I was given a full-time secretary. She was a young woman in her late twenties who had been a secretary for about five years.

In our first week on the job we had a long talk. I explained that I wouldn't be able to do my job without her help and her insights. "I don't think of you as a secretary who just does the stuff that I set out," I said. "I think of you as a team member. In fact, I want to change your title from secretary to 'administrative assistant.'

"Yes, I'll be your boss, but essentially I want you to run everything. My role will be to coach you, to support and encourage you. Together, let's develop a policy manual that will answer the questions likely to be raised by students or faculty members. Then we won't have to keep guessing at what we decided last time or what we need to say to new faculty or students."

It was fun to watch her reaction. She was surprised, pleased and a little bit afraid of the new responsibility, but she was glad for the challenge. It was also interesting to watch her relate to other women at the university who held only secretarial positions. She was no longer *just* a secretary. She was now an "administrative assistant."

At the beginning of each new class, as program director I took the opportunity to welcome the students and assure them we were very concerned about their success in the program. Then I stepped aside and let the administrative assistant explain the nuts and bolts of the campus, of working in the program and of their working with her.

A distinct change occurred in the students' and the professors' attitudes toward this newly-appointed administrative assistant. They saw her as a person of real power—a person who was a vital link to their success. This ended up as a win-win situation all around: for the students and profs, who got good assistance, for the young woman, who grew into a very responsible position, and for me, as I could delegate much of my work to her with confidence.

You may not be the boss who can bestow titles and upgrade responsibilities, but you can respect and affirm women in every relationship you have. Don't let the harassment issue make you afraid of women. This is a great opportunity for you to get on the bandwagon toward making our business and educational worlds, professions and marriages stronger because of women's powerful and insightful input.

PART THREE

Insights for Women to Reduce Harassment

14
What Women Need to *Know* to Reduce Harassment

Many women, unfortunately, are passive victims of harassment at work, in the professions and in education. They hope "it" will go away. They keep telling themselves that men don't really mean anything by it.

Women harassed by their husbands keep thinking that it will get better; he will change somehow. And the woman in the dating world hopes he won't do it again or that another man will come into her life, automatically knowing what she wants and where her boundaries are.

Women have been taught to be congenial and helpful. These normally positive traits can work against them and translate into a passivity which makes them victims.

Some women act like our cat, Mon Amie. When a more powerful cat comes into our yard, she freezes in her tracks. If the cat moves closer to her, she rolls over on her back to indicate submissiveness. Sadly, some women have been conditioned to be afraid, and their only reaction in the face of sexual harassment is submissiveness.

Passive women will continue to be harassed. One way out of harassment is to eliminate passivity, and passivity can be partly eliminated by expanding your knowledge.

We hope you're gaining a broader understanding of men, yourself and the harassment issue as you've come this far in the book. Now let's focus on a few more insights that will help you move from passivity and fear to a healthy balance of cooperation and assertiveness in your male relationships.

What Turns Men On

Some women foolishly expose themselves to sexual harassment because they don't know what ignites a man's fire. What does hit his "hot" button? What are the things that make him become more aggressive and potentially a sexual harasser?

Let's start with the concept that harassment works both ways. Men feel they are harassed by women! They say women lead them on through dress, flirtatious looks and sexual remarks.

A Live Example

I (Jim) was in a local copy shop, picking up some work they had done for us. A new employee dress code had recently gone into effect. All the employees were now fairly well dressed: that is, the men were wearing ties and dress slacks and the women were in dresses or skirts—no blue jeans.

The young woman who waited on me was in her late twenties. Since my order was not quite finished, I stood at the counter waiting. Then I began to notice all of the other employees interacting with this young woman as they worked at various machines.

She had on a very lacy black dress with an uneven hemline that varied from her knees to her ankles. She was a strikingly pretty young woman and had a terrific figure. I know she had a great figure because as she stood at a machine sideways in front of me, I could see that she didn't have a slip on. Her well-formed legs were visible all the way up to her black panties. Her full bust line and black bra were also easy to see through the filmy dress material.

I found myself fighting the urge to stare at her. I shifted my attention to watching other men in the shop. Two of the employees who stood nearest to her were talking very rapidly to each other and to her. I had watched these guys on many other occasions, and ordinarily they were cool and very businesslike.

Today their faces were flushed with excitement. One was talking about his wife and their recent marriage, and the other was talking about his girlfriend. I had the distinct feeling that their comments about the women in their lives were to protect themselves from their understandable fascination with this young woman's body.

Without being too obvious, I gradually turned and looked around the shop at the other male employees and customers. There were about a dozen other men in the shop. Some were working, while others were waiting for orders to be copied. Without exception, each one had positioned himself so that he was able to look up over his work and take in the sight of this pretty young woman in her flimsy black dress.

I looked at the young woman's face—especially her eyes. They were not hard, nor were they the provocative eyes of a prostitute. I really thought, *she probably grew up on an Iowa farm.*

Then I realized that this attractive young woman was probably trying, in her own way, to match the dress code of the organization. But she didn't have the faintest, faintest clue that she was turning the eyes and pumping the hearts of all the men in that shop.

Don't Fan the Flames

Yes, men must take responsibility—but women should not unnecessarily light fires. You can avoid some sexual harassment by knowing that men are turned on differently than women. Men are very visual and have short fuses. Watch the way you dress.

Let's get specific. Don't go braless. Don't wear tight-fitting clothes. If you have a choice, wear a longer rather than a shorter skirt. And don't wear clothes that people can see through or low necklines that men can look down into when you lean over.

Don't talk about sex scenes in movies or tell sexually oriented jokes. It's wrong for men and it's wrong for women. Sometimes women try to show they are equal by talking as dirty as men. This approach only demeans a women and plays into men's hands.

Sensual comments and actions lead men on. Remember they are already oversexualizing all you say and do. Don't perch on the edge of a man's desk with your legs crossed. He thinks you're asking him to respond.

Remember how men have been *socialized*. They're not trained to succeed in the world through relationships, as are women. They are socialized to compete, succeed and be aggressive.

In addition, men not only tend to *sexualize* everything in life, but (studies have shown) many men think of sex or sexually related items as often as every few minutes.

Remember also not to surrender *power* to a man in a love relationship. Your love and commitment to each other should grow in small, equal increments. If one of you loves the other more, there is the possibility that the one who loves less will manipulate the one who loves more.

Keep your eyes on the fact that God has created you with special abilities. And God has long-term plans for you, if you cooperate with his loving direction. Don't short-circuit God's special gifting in your life by giving a man unequal power because you love him more than he loves you.

Weakness Is Bait for Him

You need to understand that if a woman acts weak, she tends to invite harassment. This is often seen in the workplace where a man with more power may be tempted to harass a woman of lesser power. If the power role is reversed, the man is less likely to harass the same woman. You may not have the power of position, but you can be in control of yourself and the outcome of a harassing event.

Sadly, as a woman gains power and prestige, she is likely to be called a "bitch." Remember, this is the man's problem, unless a woman is now becoming exploitative, flaunting her new power position.

A woman's weakness is also destructive in marriage. If she does not talk to her husband about what she likes or doesn't like, if she does not help him grow up, if she continues to yield to his harassment, then, strangely, he will tend to mistreat her even more.

An exploited married woman, doing all the servant's jobs without saying anything about the inequity, will likely be constantly harassed. It's almost as if the man is punishing her for not being a full woman or his equal, even though he is part of the reason she isn't.

We've Seen It Happen

Sally and I had flown to the East Coast to lead a marriage enrichment seminar for a very large church. We arrived the evening before the seminar and were met at the airport by the senior pastor and his executive secretary. She was a very intelligent and attractive woman who was fifteen years younger than he.

As the four of us waited for the luggage to be delivered from the plane, Sally and I couldn't help noticing the pastor and secretary's obvious enjoyment of each other. Sally's eyes met mine. I knew what she was thinking, and she knew my mind as well.

This pastor explained the important role of his executive secretary in the church. He said, "She's my indispensable right hand. She always seems to know what needs to be done. She makes me look good."

He then turned to Sally and started congratulating her about the impact that she was making in the world. "You're on radio and television. You travel all around the country. You're writing books and articles. And still you keep up with all the responsibilities of being a wife and mother. You're leading a wonderful life," he purred charmingly.

After they dropped us off at the hotel and while we were getting settled into our room, I said to Sally, "You just watch. When we meet this pastor's wife, she's going to be a beaten-down, harassed, shriveled little woman. I'll bet he has exploited and abused her. Yet he so deeply appreciates powerful women like his secretary and you."

We didn't see the pastor's wife through the whole weekend until Sunday morning when she meekly came to meet us after the morning service. Sure enough, she looked dowdy and fifteen years older than her real age. Her demeanor and words showed that she was a shriveled person who didn't have a shred of self-confidence. She had nothing to say other than a mild, "Thank you for being here."

We wondered how this woman felt about the continued lavish praise directed to other women by her husband. Perhaps she was the product of two forces—a harassing husband who withheld love and her own passivity. Sadly, it appeared that the more he caused her to shrink, the more he despised her.

About a year later we heard that this "successful pastor" (but unsuccessful husband) had divorced his wife and left the ministry.

As a woman, you must not be passive at work, in your profession, on dates or in your marriage. We're not at all suggesting that you be obnoxiously aggressive. You don't have to be hostile in order to convince people you are a confident and thoughtful person with a contribution to make. And you certainly don't have to make sexual remarks to show you can play the game like the men! Your full personhood will be seen if you are assertive when necessary, but not constantly aggressive. People will like you better and men will respect you more.

Capitalize on the Differences

Most men process life from a *task* point of view, whereas women process life from a *relationship* viewpoint. Understanding that distinction will help you see both the limitation and importance of men.

Seeing how the two sexes process life and information differently should help you understand that as a woman you have an important contribution to make to the world in general and to men in particular. Many men may see *only* the facts. You can offer the relationship orientation such a man needs—even if he doesn't realize it! However, remember that you also tend to have a limitation; you may see *only* the relationships and never get around to the facts or the task.

Men are not born superior. Yes, they do some things better than women, but women do some things better than men. Men need your insights and contributions in order to be balanced. Don't try to be like a man. Keep offering your female insights and perspectives to give wholeness to men and the world.

Value Him

Above all else, men need one basic thing. No, it's not sex! If you ask men, they might say sex is their basic need—but it's not! *A man's basic need is to be respected.*

Inside each man is an insecure little boy who wonders if he's measuring up, if he's doing a good job, if people like him. When you understand this basic need in a man, you can take positive action by building his self-image.

At first, in a working situation, he may interpret your respect and admiration as a desire for sexual closeness. But you can also go on the "positive offensive" by letting him know that you value him as a person and want to be his friend, but you're not at all interested in an affair or a date.

Men need affirmation from women. They get some affirmation from other men, but there is a refreshing honesty in a woman's affirmation. A few close relationships between men are based on honesty, but all too frequently men are affirmed to the advantage of the person doing the affirming. In other words, a boss may compliment a middle manager, knowing that by praising him he is going to get more production out of him, not because he is his friend or wants the best for his life.

A woman has a great opportunity to strengthen the men in her life—her husband, sons, boss, fellow employees, friends. They will believe her affirmation, if she doesn't manipulate but genuinely wants to help build them up.

Mixing Fun with Respect

Balance is the goal for all of your relationships with men. You can poke fun at them, but also remember to praise them. You must help them laugh at themselves, but you also need to admire their strengths.

The current jokes show the continued misunderstandings and exploitation of both men and women. But perhaps laughing about our differences is a good step toward better understanding.

The "dumb men jokes" that have been in vogue recently illustrate the way a woman can playfully make fun of the weaknesses in a man. Enjoy these:

"What's the difference between government bonds and men? Bonds mature."

"How do you force that man of yours to do sit-ups? Put the TV remote control between his toes."

"What does a man consider a seven-course meal? Hot dog and a six-pack."

"Why is it a good thing that there are women astronauts? When the crew gets lost in space, someone will ask directions."

"So, you know why dumb-blonde jokes are one-liners? So men can understand them!"[1]

But don't forget the praise and the appreciation. Don't let the jokes trap you in an arrogance that becomes a backlash against men. Don't become a "man basher." Rather, learn all you can about men so that you become best friends, best lovers, best marriage partners, best coworkers and best professional colleagues.

15

What Women Need to *Be* to Reduce Harassment

A few months ago, one of the women in my (Sally's) small Bible study group asked what project Jim and I were working on. "We're writing a book about sexual harassment," I responded. After a pause, I asked if any of them ever ran into harassment.

They told me some stories and, finally, one of my friends said, "I think a lot of it depends on the woman. If you're poised and willing to say no, men respect that. But if you're not sure of yourself, men seem to have an uncanny ability to pick that up. So the key thing is to be sure of yourself and come across as the person in charge." My other friends agreed with her.

Women who are *self-assured,* who have *secure boundaries* and who are not carrying a lot of *emotional baggage* from their past seem to be the women who are less frequently harassed.

Self-Assured—Winning the War Within

Women with low self-images have a driving urgency to do better, try harder and please more. Every woman who feels inadequate ultimately wants to be perfect and have everything around her perfect so that people will love and respect her. Of course, she fails, because no one is perfect and every situation has flaws. Intellectually she understands that, but she keeps trying to do the impossible. As a result, she struggles with many of the following issues as she tries to be better—to be perfect.

Insecurity. The recurring theme of perfectionists is insecurity. "Who am I? Am I worthy of being loved? If I try a little harder or am a little more perfect, will I finally be accepted?" Insecurity plagues a woman, driving her to work harder to please more. Bosses, husbands and men in dating relationships love this quality. And men are likely to harass her because of her insecurity.

Control. Insecurity also drives a woman to try to control all of life. Unconsciously her mind is saying, "If I can perfectly control my environment, my relationships, and responsibilities—then I can be in a power position and I'll feel more secure."

On the surface this desire to be perfectly in control seems like a wonderful idea, but it has a definite downside. One woman put her finger on it very precisely when she said, "I don't try anything unless I can get an A."

Fear of Risk. The insecure woman or perfectionist is not willing to risk. Everything has to be guaranteed ahead of time. She chooses to stay out of new relationships because they might eventually fall apart. So she decides to be alone rather than risk failure. It's easy for harassment to happen to the woman who is afraid to risk losing. She thinks, "If I speak up, I might lose my job."

Frequently an insecure woman stays in a career where she is safe, rather than risk new opportunities. One woman told us, "I am highly critical of myself and others. Consequently, I'm often disappointed by the actions of others and I withdraw quickly for fear of repeated disappointment. My fear keeps me at a distance from people, and that damages *all* my relationships—with peers, colleagues and friends."

Never Enough. For the insecure woman, enough is never enough. She is never satisfied to be the first or the best. No matter what the accomplishments have been, she still feels empty inside. She thinks, "Maybe if I try a little more, I'll feel good about myself." But "more" is never enough. Insecurity is an internal problem not ultimately helped by more success.

Fear of Intimacy. The insecure woman has difficulty in being intimate and vulnerable. She is afraid she won't be liked if someone knows very much about her.

I (Jim) know from my own experience the fear of revealing my weaknesses. Sometimes I tell a group, "I'm going to introduce myself to you first by telling you about my degrees, my books and articles, my travels around the world and other achievements." Then I go on to also tell them about my dysfunctional childhood and how inadequate and insecure I feel because of it.

Finally I ask, "With which person would it be easier to share a problem—the successful one or the one who feels weak?" People have always felt closer to the weak Jim.

My first tendency, however, is to impress them with my accomplishments, with the result that they can't get close to me. I've finally learned that it's easier for people to relate to me when I reveal some of my shortcomings, rather than only my successes. They see me as more human.

Anger. Another trait of women with a low self-image is anger. The anger is linked to *inadequacy* ("Why should I be so inferior and unable to be what I want to be?") and the *inability to control life* ("Why can't I make life and people be the way they *should* be?") The angry woman may hide behind a victim mentality and always have endless reasons for her anger. She feels cheated; she envies others.

Yet life can never be perfect. Nobody has everything. If you are angry, we suggest that you let your anger energize you toward steps of personal growth, such as returning to school to prepare for a better job, reading books on self-image, spending time in a small sharing group or investing in private counseling.

Guilt. In addition, women with a low self-image frequently feel guilty for not being perfect and for not being able to control events so life turns out right. On top of the guilt they feel for being imperfect, they also feel guilty for getting angry at themselves, at other people and at God.[1]

Improving Your Self-Image

Let's think together about the process of improving your self-image so that you reduce the likelihood of harassment. The following steps will become practical building blocks for this process.

Building a strong self-image requires that you become a reflective person. Dr. Alan Knox has some guidance on how to be reflective: "Devote time to unstructured solitude . . . be willing to daydream and speculate, be reflective, consider strengths and weaknesses, along with problems, [and] opportunities . . . be willing to express feelings. Allow the mind to freely associate with such phrases as 'I'd like to,' 'I choose to,' 'I have to,' 'I'm afraid to,' or 'I can't.' "[2]

As you become a reflective woman, you will more accurately understand who you are. Then you will be able to modify those areas which can be changed and learn to work within your limitations, realizing that you are totally known and greatly loved by your ultimate Friend—God.

Let us suggest a little project that we've used with hundreds of people as they have worked to develop stronger self-esteem. Start by making lists in the following areas:

1. *All the things I like to do.* List things that are pleasant and

fun for you. Remember, no one else has to see this list, so be as honest as possible. Try to include fifty to one hundred items. Develop this list over several days. Maybe your list will include items such as walking in the rain, listening to country music, biking, running barefoot in the park. Don't be afraid to include crazy stuff that may be known only to you.

2. *All the things I am able to do.* List all of the areas in which you have skills and abilities, even if some of these skills are just developing. You might list things you know a lot about that you could share with other people, such as how to transplant a tree, ski, swim, make great omelettes. List everything, even if it seems small or unimportant. Remember, you don't have to show your list to anyone else.

3. *The most negative influences, events or people in my life.* List the "downers" for you. Remember, it's impossible to forgive any person or even God unless you first acknowledge that the incident or situation is a problem for you. Don't cover up. Again, remember this is your private list.

4. *The most positive influences, events or people in my life.* List the special people or events that have made favorable contributions to your life. Then jot a word or two about how these influenced you.

5. *I am most angry at . . .* This list might include world events, people, situations or lifestyles. List the items that really anger you.

6. *I am most happy with . . .* Now list the things that produce happiness and joy in you.

7. *Before I die I want to . . .* List all the things you hope to accomplish before you die.

We realize that you're not going to whip off these lists all at once. In fact, that's not the best way to do it. Take several days to work on this project.

You'll notice patterns developing. You'll see the dominant factors, both negative and positive, that have formed your life.

You'll also begin to spot forces and people that energize your life in positive or negative ways. These items will give you important information about who you are.

As you go through the lists, notice that some items are very similar and indicate strong tendencies in your personality. Make sure that you actually incorporate these desires, abilities and dreams into your overall lifestyle and relationships. You must live out the dreams and patterns that are shown on your lists or you will experience a discomfort with yourself that may even verge on hostility, anger or depression.[3]

As you begin to value yourself, to see God's unique creation in you and to sense your unique contribution to the world, you should be able to say to yourself the following five statements:

☐ I belong; I am wanted; I do have a place in the world and with people.

☐ I have worth; I do count for something; I can respect myself.

☐ I am competent; I can do certain things, maybe not everything, but I am competent to do some things.

☐ I have moral and ethical standards; I know what is right; I do have internal values; I am not a victim or a puppet.

☐ I do make a difference; I can influence and change situations and people.[4]

Carefully Define Your Boundaries

Low self-esteem is directly tied to your understanding of where your territory stops and someone else's starts. This is called a boundary issue. Harassed women not only have low self-esteem; they don't know how to establish their own boundaries or to honor another person's boundaries. This makes them likely targets for harassers.

One of the best discussions of boundaries is found in the book *Facing Co-dependence*. The author, Pia Mellody, says, "Boundary systems are invisible and symbolic fences." These fences have three purposes:

1. to keep people from coming into our space and abusing us
2. to keep us from going into their space and abusing them
3. to give each of us a way to identify who we are

Then she talks about two types of boundaries, external and internal. Our external boundary is a combination of physical and sexual distance. Our external boundary controls how close we let people come to us and whether they may touch us or not.

Our internal boundary protects our thinking, feelings and behaviors and separates *our* thoughts, *our* feelings and *our* actions from those of other people.

Pia Mellody says, "Our internal boundary also stops us from taking responsibility for the thoughts, feelings, and behaviors of others. These boundaries keep us from being manipulated by other people. Boundaries also keep us from controlling those around us."[5]

Boundary Problems Are Connected to Power
Other writers have described the boundary issue by thinking of themselves as inside a tent with a zipper around the door. The question is asked, "Is the control for the zipper on the inside of the tent or the outside?" Individuals with boundary problems tend to allow other people to control the zipper.[6]

Ideal boundaries are not rigid walls but are flexible like movable partitions. Even in the most intimate relationships, there should be flexible boundaries as people change.

Jim and I are married, but still I am Sally and he is Jim. We have three daughters, three sons-in-law and several grandchildren. Each individual has his or her own boundary definition. We cannot live life for our children or grandchildren. If we intrude into their lives, or they into ours, frustration follows—and maybe fireworks as well! Fortunately, we continue to learn new and better ways to respect each other's boundaries. As we do, we actually find more freedom and fulfillment in our relationships.

Dysfunction and Self-Esteem

In *Adult Children: The Secrets of Dysfunctional Families,* John
and Linda Frill say,

> In a healthy family, children's needs for security, warmth,
> nurturance, and guidance are met most of the time. These
> children enter adulthood with a sense of security and trust
> that is *inside* themselves.
>
> In dysfunctional families, these needs are not met enough
> or at all, and these children enter adulthood with a sense of
> incompleteness, mistrust, and fear *inside* themselves, along
> with a strong need for some kind of security *outside* them-
> selves.
>
> As adults who grew up in troubled families, we constantly
> seek to fill up the empty parts inside of us that were never
> met while we were growing up, and it is the *external* search
> for our unmet needs that leads us into addictive lifestyles.[7]

So Now What?

Your own sense of security and control are very important to
protect you from sexual harassment. If you are unsure of yourself, get some help. Read books that will help you develop your
self-image.[8] Be around people who affirm you rather than cut
you down.

Joining the right small group can help. Practice self-assertive-
ness. Perhaps you need to see a wise counselor or therapist.
Don't be afraid to do what you need to do. Part of being in
control of your life is getting the help you need.

16
What Women Need to *Do* to Reduce Harassment

Edwin is the manager of a small Christian bookstore that is part of a national chain of bookstores. Ed, as he'd rather be called, is in his middle fifties and is a very pleasant, friendly man. But he thinks as many men his age do: women are useful objects but aren't equal to men, and this harassment thing is ridiculous.

Judith, a woman in her late forties, is one of several employees. She has been an executive secretary for many years in other businesses and is this store's secretary and bookkeeper. Both Ed and Judith have worked at the store for fewer than three years. Judith has come to see Ed as a gigantic pain.

Ed would totally reject the idea that he is a harasser. He thinks of himself as friendly. "I just want to get to know my employees so we have a close working relationship and I know better how to pray for them."

Ed's comment, taken at face value, seems harmless enough. However, Judith began to notice that more than half of Ed's conversations with her focused on non-job-related concerns. At first, Judith thought he was just nosy. Then she recognized a disturbing pattern in their conversations. For example, when one of her grandchildren was born, Ed asked if the mother was going to breast-feed the child. Judith felt funny. "What does breast-feeding have to do with my job here at the store?" she wondered.

Even though she felt strange, she made a quick response of "Yes," hoping that would be the end. But he persisted, "Children need to be nursed. They need to feel their mother's breast against their face, to suck on her nipple and to feel her arms around them."

Judith was boiling inside. "This guy is fantasizing. This is none of his business. I don't want to share my family's personal life with this man. How can I get him off my back?"

Ed continued to bring up other personal things. He asked what she and her husband did during their evenings, where they spent vacations, what her favorite restaurants were and what her husband did for her that made her feel loved.

Every time these things came up, Judith was infuriated. She had the feeling that Ed was not really asking about her husband but was trying to learn more about her personal tastes and feelings. She suspected that if she allowed her emotional door to be opened even a crack to Ed, he would move through with more personal questions and suggestions. She felt very uncomfortable. It seemed to her that Ed was continually trying to create a sexual environment, hoping Judith would respond.

It Gets Worse

Ordinarily, Ed ate a quick brown-bag lunch in his office so that he could keep working. But soon he started going to the same little coffee shop where Judith ate lunch. He startled her the first time he showed up. His excuse was, "I forgot my lunch today, and sometimes I just get tired of brown-bagging it. Do you mind if I sit here with you?"

Yes, I mind, Judith said to herself. But her second reaction was, *This guy's my boss. Everyone else seems to think he's harmless. But why does he give me the creeps?*

Ed started forgetting his brown-bag lunch more and more often until, finally, Judith changed to a different restaurant. In a few days, Ed showed up there. He was fairly direct: "I missed you at the other place. Having lunch with you was a bright spot in my day."

Having lunch with me? Judith thought. *I was just enduring this guy! What do I have to do to get loose from him?*

Ed made flattering comments to Judith in the office and at the various restaurants where he would track her down. He said he was glad for the positive addition she was in his life as well as in the store. He commented about her clothes, hair, eyes, fingernails and perfume. "There's a radiance about you. I just feel wonderful when I see your face or look out through my office window and see you sitting there."

This was clear-cut sexual harassment. Judith decided she had to *do* something.

Hard to Nail Down

Subtle harassment of this type is very widespread. And many times it's difficult to put your finger on it, so it frequently goes unchallenged. To many men, this kind of behavior isn't harassment, it's just ordinary friendship.

But, beyond any question at all, Ed had established a sexually harassing environment. Judith dreaded coming to work. She liked the job and she needed the money, but she hated having Ed in her life. She started planning ways that she could avoid seeing Ed. But he kept pursuing her.

Just because this low-level sexual harassment is common

doesn't mean we should let it go on. Low-level harassment, in some ways, is even more damaging psychologically to women than if a man asks very directly for sex. That can anger a woman sufficiently so that she will say "No!" and perhaps even follow with a threat of her own: "If you don't back off, I'm going to talk to personnel and you'll be out of here."

Subtle harassment, however, is likely to be ignored or excused. "Maybe it's just my perception," a woman thinks. "Certainly he didn't mean it. After all, he's such a nice man. I'm not sure what he would do if I said something."

The Power of Power

In Ed's situation, an additional issue may have been in the picture. He probably wouldn't have followed through on a full-blown affair because of his position in the Christian community, but it appears that his harassment was a subtle way of expressing his disdain for working women. He never praised Judith's good work; he only made comments about what tasks she still needed to finish. His other remarks were all in the category of subtle sexual harassment.

Ed seemed to enjoy watching Judith squirm. It gave him a sense of power when she was uncomfortable. He knew she had to be nice to him because he was the boss. Besides, he made it clear that he wrote the performance reviews that would affect her income and relationship with the bookstore chain.

Preventative Actions

Our counsel to Judith was direct. "It's okay to be angry about these intrusions into your life. You have a right to work in an environment free of sexual harassment. Take all the preventative measures you can."

We urged her to make sure the clothing she wore was very modest. We also encouraged her to watch her comments, focusing them entirely on work, not mentioning her personal life or

Ed's personal life. Also, she was to watch her actions so that she didn't present her body in any way that could be construed as alluring. Ed is still responsible—but she shouldn't deliberately cause trouble.

We advised her to continue to control the "friendship" Ed was trying to establish with her. "Avoid him at lunch. Do not answer any of his remarks about your personal life, your clothing or your body," we warned. "Tell him directly that you don't want to talk about personal or family matters."

In addition, we urged her to be informed about the sexual harassment protection that has been set by the courts in recent years. Her local library could provide that information.

We also encouraged her to explore the policy statements the bookstore chain had printed in their employee's manual. She should learn the specific language and procedural steps to eliminate harassment. In addition, we asked her to identify a woman in the personnel department at the main office whom she could call upon if Ed's harassment didn't stop.

Protective Measures to Take

We suggested to Judith that she go back over her calendar and write down a detailed chronology of all that she had shared with us. It was important that she record as closely as she could what Ed had said and, even more important, how she felt about his words and actions. Further, she should detail any future incidents of harassment if they took place.

In a _Washington Post_ article entitled "Between the Sexes, Confusion at Work," the author writes, "A bad evaluation, attempted rape, a bonus for being 'bedded'—that is well understood as harassment. But this other, this uneasy feeling some women have, this twilight zone of what's user-friendly behavior in the workplace, this shadow of fear and distrust—men generally have a hard time figuring out what the new boundaries are between the sexes. _What do women NOT want?_

"And women don't tell them. Women usually don't let on what sexual harassment is, when it happens or why it hurts, what devastating psychic damage it can do."[1]

Proactive Actions to Take

It's not enough to try to prevent sexual harassment, and it's not enough to record the harassing instances in case you ever proceed with a formal investigation or a legal suit. You also *must take action.*

Tell the harasser *exactly what it is* that is offensive to you, as we've described earlier. Don't wait until the offenses become so obnoxious that you explode with anger. Start with the very first incident when you have a "funny feeling," then speak kindly, yet directly, about what is offensive to you.

If the offensive harassment does not stop, then the offender needs to know clearly that you will take further action. Remind him that your company's management has already outlined steps for reporting sexual harassment and the repercussions for harassers.

Recovery from Harassment

Judith's situation was low-level harassment. Nevertheless, over the three-year period, she experienced many instances of being sick to her stomach. Often she wanted to quit her job. She frequently cried in the women's washroom. Other times she took out the anger she felt toward Ed on her husband.

Perhaps your situation has been even more severe. Whatever harassment you've experienced—whether low-level offensive remarks, unwanted touching or actual rape—you may need some additional help in the way of counseling or a support group. Your company or institution already may have set up the mechanism for you to get help. Don't be embarrassed to reveal your situation! Ask about counseling and recovery groups. And don't forget to ask about insurance or payments to help you to cover the cost of this process.

Your places of employment, study and social activity should be harassment-free. If they are not, it's not enough to hope it will go away. You *must take action.* You *must do something* in order to get rid of that sick feeling in the pit of your stomach and, at the same time, help other women who may be struggling with the same harassment but who might be even more afraid to speak up than you are.

PART FOUR

Values
That Enable
People to Rise
Above
Harassment

17

What You
Believe Will
Change Your Life

The two of us travel a lot in our work. When we're working on a book project, we like to talk to people along the way. On a flight for a Midwestern conference, I (Jim) got into a lively discussion about harassment with two female flight attendants. In a few minutes two other women and a male flight attendant joined the conversation. They told me story after story.

A woman attendant said, "There are several pilots on this line to whom I just hate to take food. When I open the cockpit door and say, 'Can I get you anything?' this one guy in particular always says, 'Sure! Come in and close the door. I want you.' "

The male attendant said the harassment he most objected to was people thinking that he was "gay" because he was a flight attendant. "They think it's a woman's job and they look at me the same way as they look at a guy working in a beauty shop."

By this time, they were all saying, "Yeah! Yeah!" One of them chimed in, "What really bothers me is the way people look down on you. They treat you as if you were their servant. They're so pushy and demanding. Sometimes I'd just like to smash the food into their faces. They don't seem to understand at all how difficult it is to serve people in these cramped quarters."

Another one added, "Yeah, but it's the disrespect that's the worst thing. I remember this one guy had complained about everything since he got on the plane. His food was too cold. His lettuce salad was wilted. We put too much ice in his drinks.

"Finally, after I had made several trips to serve him, he said, 'Pardon me, Miss, do you need a high-school education in order to get this job?' I tried to control myself. As calmly as I could, I responded, 'Everyone on this flight has a college degree, and two of us have master's degrees.' "

One of the attendants, who had been silent up to this point, said angrily under her breath, "I hate being treated as if I'm a piece of meat! A few months ago we had a planeload of wrestlers. Just before takeoff, I was pushing some baggage straps into the overhead compartments, and one of them poked my breast and said, "Do you mind if I take a nibble?"

When I returned to my seat and reflected on what the attendants had said, I realized all their stories followed a similar pattern. Whether it was about sexual pinching, poking and come-ons, put-downs about education or cracks about males working in this position, they all had one common theme—a degrading exploitation.

In fact, that's what harassment is basically all about. It's taking advantage of someone else. Harassment is a total disrespect of another's personhood.

Harassment in its many forms will not be resolved until we address the abuse of human values. If men and women can change the way they think about each other and the value they place on each other, harassment will disappear. So the question is, how can we change people's values—the concepts they hold as their guiding principles?

What Brings About Change?

New ideas, or new ways of thinking about an old idea, subtly change our minds and our personalities. When we expose ourselves to new ideas about old problems, an almost imperceptible change starts to take place. Therefore, to change your values, expose yourself on a regular basis to new and positive ideas about the areas in which you want to change.

Stressful events often will produce a radical value change. We are confronted with a situation that forces us to rethink our position and take action. For example, if you are aware that you've been harassed at work, or you see someone else being harassed, that stressful event—that churning in the pit of your stomach—can be your ally. It helps you to refine your ideas of what you view as important.

Group discussion also will help reinforce any changes you are making. As you hear other people talk, you may feel comfortable with some aspects of your thinking about a particular issue; that strengthens your confidence. You may feel uncomfortable about other aspects; that challenges you to reexamine and perhaps adjust your thinking.

For example, a small-group discussion of this book would be helpful to many different groups of people, such as dating couples, men and women who work together, married couples, men's and women's study groups. The group discussion puts subtle pressure on you to continue thinking about this issue. Because you meet regularly, you can't ignore the subject even if, in some instances, it's rather painful to think about.

Commitment to a higher person or principle will also change your values. For example, people are changed when they begin to mentally interact with Jesus and daily try to follow his teachings. When they decide they want their daily life to characterize the people-attitudes that Jesus exhibited, they treat people with more dignity.

These individual actions will cause powerful changes in our lives when we practice them.

A Life-Changing Model

As we read about the life of Jesus in the pages of the New Testament, we do not so much see him moving from event to event as from person to person. His attitudes and actions were in sharp contrast to the typical sexual harasser's behavior. Think about the noble way he related to people.

Respect. Harassers have little respect for people. But there are many incidents that clearly show Jesus' deep respect for all types of people. To illustrate, think about the woman who was caught in the very act of adultery by some of the religious leaders. They thought they would use her to trap Jesus.

They didn't really care about her. They only wanted a verifiable case of adultery. They wanted to push Jesus against the theological wall of the Old Testament teaching: people who commit adultery are to be stoned to death.

So now they had the perfect setup. We've always wondered how they could have arranged to trap this woman. Perhaps someone in their own religious order was willing to be the man in this scenario. It's interesting that no man was brought with her to be punished.

When they threw her before Jesus with the charge that she was an adulteress caught in the very act, he did not treat her with contempt—nor did he treat the accusers with contempt. He simply stooped to the ground and started to write something. (Our personal view is that he was jotting down the sins of the men who were standing there, waiting to stone her to death.) Then he made that great statement, "Whoever has never sinned himself, let him throw the first stone."

One by one, the men slipped away until Jesus was left alone with the woman. At that point he asked, "Where are your accusers? Doesn't anyone condemn you?" She responded, "No one, Lord."

Jesus' response is simple: "Neither do I. Go and sin no more."[1]

Jesus' respect for people is also seen when he stops his entourage of followers, looks up in a tree and calls to Zacchaeus, the crooked and unpopular tax collector, telling him that he plans to go to his house for lunch that very day.[2]

Repeatedly, Jesus was criticized because he treated "lower-class people" as equal or even superior to the religious elite. On several occasions, Jesus healed people who were outsiders to the religion of Israel. On some of these occasions, he even marveled that these people had such great faith. To one of these people he said, "I haven't seen faith like this in all the land of Israel."[3]

Touch. A harasser uses touch as a way to fulfill personal fantasy. But Jesus used touch as a way to bless. Energy went from him *to* the person so that he or she was healed, encouraged or made stronger because of his touch. On the other hand, the harasser's touch demeans, exploits, and takes energy and well-being *from* the person.

Sometimes Jesus violated the strict religious rules for touching a person. No one was to touch a leper so that the disease might not spread. On one occasion, a leper came to Jesus and said, "If you will, you can heal me." The Bible says Jesus reached out and touched the man and said, "Of course I will. Be healed." And the leprosy left him instantly![4]

If a man doesn't have a strong friendship with a particular woman, however, he ought to refrain from touching her, especially if the touch might be construed to be less holy than Jesus' touch.

Freedom. The harasser's touch, words or looks are intended to control and manipulate the victim. He hopes to use the person for his personal sexual gratification.

As Jesus connected to people, there was never a sense of control or dominance. A very wealthy, powerful young man came to Jesus and wanted to be his disciple. Jesus told him that if he chose the life of a disciple, he would need to abandon his wealth and the power inherent in that wealth. The young man weighed the decision and sorrowfully turned away.

Jesus' reaction was not to force or manipulate the young man; it was to give freedom. The young man could make his own choice, even though Jesus would rather that he choose to follow him.

Growth. In harassing situations, victims always become *less* than they are. They feel unclean, uncomfortable at work, distrustful of people, and they blame themselves. But as Jesus associated with people, he always had the purpose of helping them become whole.

The major focus of his time on earth was to train and equip people, to deliver them from the limitations of their past and to help them see what they could be in the future. Those incidents ranged from helping humble fishermen with limited vision to become his apostles and writers of New Testament books, all the way to changing powerful men such as the wealthy Joseph of Arimathea who provided Jesus' burial ground. Every one of these people became more than they ever thought they could be.

Modeling the manner in which Jesus related to people would eliminate harassment from the workplace, education, medicine, the military, dating, religion, marriage and any place where harassment's ugly head is seen.

A good test of whether your actions, or someone else's actions toward you, are harassment is to ask, "Would Jesus have related in this way?"

The Greatest of All

During the final earthly hours that Jesus spent with his disciples, he carried out a shocking act of servitude. He was their leader, teacher and model. He was God right there in the flesh. Yet he took a basin of water and, person by person, washed their feet—including those of Judas who would betray him.

Foot washing was supposed to be done by a servant, but this was a private meeting because of the political and religious animosity toward Jesus. Therefore, no servants were present to do the menial task of washing dusty feet. None of the disciples moved to do it, but Jesus, the Creator and Sustainer of the universe, did.

Jesus' act of serving not only shocked the disciples but also grabbed their attention so he could explain his purpose. He performed this lowly task to teach them, and us, that we all are to serve each other.[5] The truly great person is not the one who is served as the boss, the head, the president—the "hot dog." The truly great person is the one who serves.

What you believe *will* change your thinking, your attitudes and, ultimately, your actions. As you understand and model the way Jesus related to people, you will build people up rather than harass them. Your contacts with people will take on a positive aspect that will help others to become whole people and to develop deep, genuine relationships with you and others.[6]

One Thing I Want

Alex B. Thompson is an extremely wealthy Danish man. He was born in Copenhagen, Denmark, but now lives on the French Riviera. He regularly is involved in multimillion-dollar transactions.

Mr. Thompson is ninety-four years old and wants to leave something so that the world will remember him. Even though he is one of the richest men in the world, he fears not being remembered.

So he asked the city of Copenhagen to name a street after him. He was willing to pay the city forty-one million dollars for any inconvenience caused by the renaming process.

The city council turned him down. They have a policy of only naming streets after famous people such as Hans Christian Andersen.

Alex Thompson was interviewed by ABC News and spoke of his sadness. He has all this money but he may not be remembered. One of his statements touched us with a deep sadness: "It's too late to be great."

He has focused his life's energy on power and money, not on people. Yes, he is a powerful and wealthy man, but he is likely to be remembered only because the city of Copenhagen turned him down. Sadly, at the end of his life he finally realizes it's too late to do something for the world.[7]

What a great investment it will be if we each get our values aligned now. Then we—and others whose lives we've touched—will have no regrets when our life ends.

Notes

Chapter 1: It's Real & It's Pervasive

[1] *National Review* 44 (July 20, 1992): 14.

[2] Andrea Stone, "Tailhook: Boom Starts Lowering," *USA Today,* Apr. 29, 1993, p. 3A; Norman Kempster, "What Really Happened at Tailhook Convention; Scandal: The Pentagon Report Graphically Describes How Fraternity-Style Hi-Jinks Turned into Hall of Horrors," *Los Angeles Times,* Apr. 24, 1993, part A, p. 1, col. 5.

[3] Peter Cary and Jim Impoco, "Many Officers, Not Many Gentlemen," *U.S. News & World Report,* 114 (May 3, 1993): 44, 49.

[4] *USA Today,* Friday, Oct. 2, 1992, p. 6A.

[5] Patricia Edmonds, "Year Later, Harassment's Real to More People: Hill Hearings Helped Change Nation's View," *USA Today,* Oct. 2, 1992, p. 6A.

[6] Alice Ann R. Head and George L. Head, "Defining Sexual Harassment," *Property and Casualty/Risk and Benefits Management,* Sept. 14, 1992.

[7] Allanna M. Sullivan, "Women Endure Job-Related Sexual Abuse," *Parade Magazine,* Aug. 16, 1981, p. 8.

[8] *Parade Magazine,* Nov. 17, 1991, p. 8.

[9] Ibid.

[10] Walter Lucas and Henry Gottlieb, "Harassment, Havoc for Employers: Latest Ruling Charts New Law on Liability and Proof," *New Jersey Law Journal,* Apr. 27, 1992, p. 1.

Chapter 2: Sexual Harassment in the Workplace

[1] Kathleen Decker, "Women Tell of Frustration in Combating Sexual Harassment," *Los Angeles Times,* Nov. 15, 1991, p. 3.

[2] Ibid.

[3] Ibid.

[4] Personal letter from Linda Doll, Downers Grove, Ill., Apr. 21, 1993.

[5] "Taking It Personally," *Washington Post,* Oct. 11, 1991.

[6] Pat Brennan and Donna Davis, "Cops Accused of Sex Harassment, *Orange County Register,* Sept. 25, 1992, p. 1; Jonathan Volzke et al., "Harassment Suit Rocks Newport Police," *Orange County Register,* Sept. 26, 1992, pp.

B1, B4.
⁷Ibid., p. B4.
⁸Ibid., pp. B1, B4.
⁹Bill Carlino, *National Restaurant News,* 26 (June 1, 1992): 58.
¹⁰Ibid.

Chapter 3: Sexual Harassment on Dates
¹A. Amick and K. Calhoun, "Resistance of Sexual Aggression: Personality, Attitudinal and Situational Factors," *Archives of Sexual Behavior* 16 (1987): 153; see also M. P. Koss, "Hidden Rape: Sexual Aggression and Victimization in a National Sample of Students in Higher Education," in *Violence in Dating Relationships,* ed. M. Pirog-Good & J. Stets (New York: Praeger, 1989); B. Miller and J. Marshall, "Coercive Sex on the University Campus," *Journal of College Student Personnel* 28 (1987): 38-47; C. Muehlenhard and M. Linton, "Date Rape and Sexual Aggression in Dating Situations: Incidence and Risk Factors," *Journal of Counseling Psychology* 36 (1987): 186-96.
²M. P. Koss and C. Oros, "Sexual Experiences Survey: A Research Instrument Investigating Sexual Aggression and Victimization," *Journal of Consulting and Clinical Psychology* 50 (1982): 456.
³R. Warshaw, *I Never Called It Rape: The "Ms." Report on Recognizing, Fighting and Surviving Date and Acquaintance Rape* (New York: Harper & Row, 1988).
⁴*New York Times,* Nov. 7, 1991, section A, p. 20.
⁵E. J. Kannin and S. R. Parcell, "Sexual Aggression: A Second Look at the Offended Female," *Archives of Sexual Behavior* 6 (1977): 67-76.
⁶B. Lott, M. Reily and D. Howard, "Sexual Assault and Harassment: A Campus Community Case Study," *Journal of Women in Culture and Society* 8 (1982): 296-319; see also N. Malamuth, "Rape Proclivity Among Males," *Journal of Social Issues* 37 (1981): 138-57.
⁷M. P. Koss, C. A. Gidycz and N. Wisniewski, "The Scope of Rape: Incidence and Prevalence of Sexual Aggression and Victimization in a National Sample of Higher Education Students," *Journal of Consulting and Clinical Psychology* 55 (1987): 163.
⁸Tracy D. Bostwick and Janice L. Delucia, "Effects of Gender and Specific Dating Behaviors on Perception of Sex Willingness and Date Rape," *Journal of Social and Clinical Psychology* 11 (1992): 22.
⁹Colette Bouchez, "Communication Between the Sexes: An Old Problem Carries New Implications," *Orange County Register,* Sept. 10, 1987, section J, p. 1.
¹⁰Ibid.
¹¹Ibid.
¹²Derrick R. Holcomb, Linda C. Holcomb, K. Annie Sondag and Nancy

Williams, "Attitudes About Date Rape: Gender Differences Among College Students," *College Student Journal* 25 (1991): 437.
[13]Ibid.
[14]R. Lance Shotland, "A Theory of the Causes of Courtship Rape: Part 2," *Journal of Social Issues* 48 (1992): 139.
[15]S. Boeringer, C. Shehan and R. Akers, "Social Contexts and Social Learning in Sexual Coercion and Aggression: Assessing the Contribution of Fraternity Membership," *Family Relations* 40 (1991): 58-64.
[16]Shotland, "A Theory of the Causes of Courtship Rape," p. 139.
[17]G. R. Riemer, *Dialogue: Dating and Marriage* (New York: Holt, Rinehart and Winston, 1968), p. 9.
[18]Bostwick and Delucia, "Effects of Gender."
[19]Steven Stack and Mary Jeanne Kanavy, "The Effect of Religion on Forcible Rape: A Structural Analysis," *Journal For Scientific Study of Religion* 22 (1983): 67-74.
[20]Daniel 11:32 KJV, with "exploits" translated by the authors as "great deeds."

Chapter 4: Sexual Harassment in Marriage

[1]John 13:13-17.
[2]For more understanding of the meaning of *headship,* see Gilbert Bilezikian, *Beyond Sex Roles* (Grand Rapids, Mich.: Baker, 1985), pp. 157-62.
[3]1 Corinthians 12:4-28.
[4]Jerry and Barbara Cook, *Choosing to Love* (Ventura, Calif.: Regal, 1982), p. 57.

Chapter 5: Sexual Harassment in Education

[1]Abigail Trafford, "Between the Sexes, Confusion at Work: Harassment Is Widespread and Its Effects Are Long-lasting," *Washington Post,* Oct. 15, 1992, Health Section, p. 8.
[2]Liz McMillen, "Many Colleges Taking a New Look at Policies on Sexual Harassment," *The Chronicle of Higher Education,* Dec. 17, 1986, pp. 1, 16.
[3]*Educational Record* 62 (1981): 52-57.
[4]James Renick, "Sexual Harassment at Work: Why It Happens, What to Do About It," *Personnel Journal* 59 (1980): 658-62.
[5]David A. Katsman, *Seven Days a Week: Women and Domestic Service in Industrializing America* (New York: Oxford University Press, 1978); Carol Hymowitz and Michaele Weissman, *A History of Women in America* (New York: Bantam, 1978); Lin Farley, *Sexual Shakedown: The Sexual Harassment of Women on the Job* (New York: McGraw-Hill, 1978); Constance Backhouse and Len Cohen, *Secret Oppression: Sexual Harassment* (Toronto: Macmillan, 1979).
[6]Donna J. Benson and Gregg E. Thomson, "Sexual Harassment on a Uni-

versity Campus: The Confluence of Authority Relations, Sexual Interest and Gender Stratification," *Social Problems* 29 (1982): 236-51.

[7] *Sexual Harassment on the Job: Questions and Answers* (New York: Working Women United Institute, 1978), p. 1.

[8] Beth Schneider, "Graduate Women, Sexual Harassment and University Policy," *Journal of Higher Education* 58 (1987): 46-65.

[9] Ibid.

[10] S. Verba, J. DiNunzio and C. Spaulding, "Unwanted Attention: Report on a Sexual Harassment Survey," Report to the Faculty Council of the Faculty of Arts and Sciences, Harvard University, 1983.

[11] Testimony of Barbara Haler, member of the Illinois Task Force on Sexual Harassment, before the House Judiciary Committee, Mar. 4, 1980.

[12] Bernice R. Sandler and Associates, "Sexual Harassment: A Hidden Problem," *Educational Record* 62 (1981): 54.

[13] Ibid., p. 56.

[14] Benson and Thomson, "Sexual Harassment on a University Campus," pp. 236-51.

[15] McMillen, "Many Colleges Taking a New Look," p. 16.

[16] Ibid.

[17] Susan Essoyan, "Sexual Harassment Disclosures an Emotional Campus Issue," *Los Angeles Times,* Apr. 2, 1991, p. A5.

[18] Ibid.

[19] Renick, "Sexual Harassment at Work," p. 660.

[20] Trafford, "Between the Sexes," p. 8.

Chapter 6: Sexual Harassment in Religion

[1] Charles L. Rassieur, *The Problem Clergymen Don't Talk About* (Philadelphia: Westminster Press, 1976), p. 20.

[2] Richard Blackmon, "The Hazards of the Ministry" D.Min. diss., Fuller Theological Seminary, 1984.

[3] "Sins of the Father" *People's Weekly Magazine* 38 (July 27, 1992): 28.

[4] "Archbishop of Santa Fe Quits Amid Accusations About Sex," *New York Times,* March 20, 1993, p. 6.

[5] Gordon Legge, "Turning a Blind Eye Hurts Church," *Calgary Herald,* June 6, 1992, p. F1.

[6] Ibid.

[7] Peter Rutter, *Sex in the Forbidden Zone* (New York: Ballantine, 1989).

[8] Ibid., pp. 148-50.

[9] Ibid., pp. 152-53.

Chapter 7: Why Do Women Put Up with It?

[1] Marie C. Wilson, "Just a Day at the Office," *New York Times,* Oct. 11, 1991, p. 15.

[2]Jonathan Volzke, "Newport Police Cut a Deal," *Orange County Register,* June 11, 1993, pp. 1, 25.

[3]Donald E. Maypole and Rosemarie Skaine, "Sexual Harassment in the Workplace," *Social Work,* Sept.-Oct. 1983, pp. 385-86.

[4]Ibid.

[5]Catherine MacKinnon, *Sexual Harassment of Working Women: A Case of Sex Discrimination* (New Haven, Conn.: Yale University Press, 1979), p. xii.

[6]Evelyn Gilbert, "Employers Urged to Enact Sex Harassment Policies," *Property and Casualty/Risk and Benefits Management,* June 1, 1992, p. 39.

Chapter 8: Guidelines for the Harassed Person

[1]Trafford, "Between the Sexes," pp. 8-9.

[2]Ibid.

[3]Ibid.

[4]Ibid.

[5]Daniel Niven, "The Case of the Hidden Harassment," *Harvard Business Review,* Mar. 1992, pp. 45-50.

[6]Ibid.

[7]Gilbert, "Employers Urged to Enact Sex Harassment Policies," p. 39.

[8]Donald J. Petersen and Douglass Massengill, "Sexual Harassment: A Growing Problem in the Workplace," *Personnel Administrator* 27 (1982): 79-89.

[9]Steven Anderson, *How to Effectively Manage Sexual Harassment* (Aurora, Colo.: Anderson/Davis, 1992).

Chapter 9: Why Men Harass

[1]Jerry Adler, "There Are Still Too Many People Who Say Boys Will Be Boys," *Orange County Register,* Nov. 15, 1992, Accent, p. 1.

[2]Jill Smolowe, reported by Elaine Lafferty, "Sex with a Scorecard" *Time,* Apr. 5, 1993, Society Section, p. 41.

[3]Adler, "There Are Still Too Many People," p. 1.

[4]George Gilder, *Men and Marriage* (Gretna, La.: Pelican, 1986), pp. 21-22; see also John Money and Anke A. Ehrhardt, *Man and Woman, Boy and Girl: The Differentiation and Dimorphism of Gender Identity from Conception to Maturity* (Baltimore, Md.: Johns Hopkins University Press, 1973); Eleanor E. Maccoby and Carol N. Jacklin, *The Psychology of Sex Differences* (Palo Alto, Calif.: Stanford University Press, 1974).

[5]Karen Horney, *Feminine Psychology* (New York: Norton, 1967); Erik H. Erikson, *Identity: Youth and Crisis* (New York: Norton, 1968); Ashley Montagu, *Touching: The Human Significance of the Skin* (New York: Columbia University Press, 1971).

[6]Gilder, *Men and Marriage;* Money and Ehrhardt, *Man and Woman;* Maccoby and Jacklin, *The Psychology of Sex Differences.*

[7]Jim Conway, *Adult Children of Legal or Emotional Divorce* (Downers

Grove, Ill.: InterVarsity Press, 1990), p. 33.
[8]Ibid., pp. 58-69.
[9]Ibid.

Chapter 10: "Male Pattern Ignorance"
[1]Berke Breathed, "Outland," *Orange Country Register,* Jan. 24, 1993.
[2]Jim Conway, *Making Real Friends in a Phony World* (Grand Rapids, Mich.: Zondervan, 1989), pp. 35-37.
[3]Ibid., p. 71.
[4]Ibid. pp. 70-84.

Chapter 11: What Men Don't Know *Will* Hurt Them
[1]"Sexual Harassment: The Abuse of Power in the Workplace," *The Connecticut Law Tribune,* Apr. 6, 1992, Verbatim, p. 3.
[2]Genesis 1:31.
[3]This section was adapted from the pamphlet *Sexual Harassment at the Workplace,* published by the Alliance Against Sexual Coercion, P.O. Box 1, Cambridge, MA 02139.

Chapter 12: What Men Need to Know About Women
[1]Jim and Sally Conway, *Women in Mid-Life Crisis* (Wheaton, Ill.: Tyndale House, 1987).
[2]Sally Conway, *Menopause* (Grand Rapids, Mich.: Zondervan, 1990).
[3]Michael Morgenstern, *How to Make Love to a Woman* (New York: Ballantine Books, 1983), p. 23-24.
[4]Ibid.

Chapter 13: To Do and Not to Do
[1]Karen Selick, "We Don't Need This Nonsense: Guidelines for Ontario Lawyers Are a Combination of Malice and Idiocy," *The Vancouver Sun,* June 24, 1992, p. A17.
[2]Taken from *The American Heritage Dictionary of the English Language* (Boston, Mass.: Houghton Mifflin, 1971).
[3]Eric J. Wallach and Alyse L. Jacobson, " 'Reasonable Woman' Test Catches On," *The National Law Journal,* July 6, 1992, Business Watch, Employment Law Section (New York: New York Law Publishing Company), p. 21.
[4]Jim and Sally Conway, *Traits of a Lasting Marriage* (Downers Grove, Ill.: InterVarsity Press, 1991).
[5]Jim Conway, *Making Real Friends in a Phony World.*

Chapter 14: What Women Need to *Know* to Reduce Harassment
[1]*Los Angeles Times,* Sept. 26, 1992, section 1, p. 1.

Chapter 15: What Women Need to *Be* to Reduce Harassment

[1]Condensed and adapted from Jim Conway, *Adult Children of Legal or Emotional Divorce* (Downers Grove, Ill.: InterVarsity Press, 1990), pp. 58-61.

[2]Alan B. Knox, *Adult Development and Learning* (San Francisco: Jossey-Bass, 1977), pp. 354-55.

[3]Condensed and adapted from Jim Conway, *Making Real Friends in a Phony World,* pp. 57-63.

[4]For further information on these five traits see Erikson, *Identity: Youth and Crisis;* Stanley Coopersmith, *The Antecedents of Self-Esteem* (San Francisco: W. H. Freeman, 1967); and Keith and Gladys Hunt, *Not Alone* (Grand Rapids, Mich.: Zondervan, 1985).

[5]Pia Mellody, *Facing Co-dependence* (San Francisco: Harper & Row, 1989), pp. 11-13.

[6]Merlea Fossum and Marilyn J. Mason, *Facing Shame: Families in Recovery* (New York: Norton, 1986), p. 71.

[7]John and Linda Friel, *Adult Children: The Secrets of Dysfunctional Families* (Deerfield Beach, Fla.: Health Communications, 1988), pp. 71-72.

[8]For example, see Josh McDowell, *Building Your Self-Esteem* (Wheaton, Ill.: Tyndale House, 1984).

Chapter 16: What Women Need to *Do* to Reduce Harassment

[1]Trafford, "Between the Sexes," p. 9.

Chapter 17: What You Believe Will Change Your Life

[1]John 8:1-11.

[2]Luke 19.

[3]Matthew 8:10, Living Bible.

[4]Luke 5:13, Living Bible.

[5]John 13:1-17; Matthew 23:11-12.

[6]Some of these thoughts are also found in Jim and Sally Conway, *Traits of a Lasting Marriage,* pp. 171-73.

[7]ABC Evening News, Mar. 10, 1993.

Jim Conway, Ph.D., and Sally Christon Conway, M.S.

Jim and Sally are cofounders of *Mid-Life Dimensions/Christian Living Resources, Inc.*, a California-based organization that offers help to people struggling to save or rebuild their marriages.

Jim and Sally speak together at colleges, seminaries, churches and retreat centers. They also appear on many radio and television programs. Besides their own books, they have contributed to many other books and magazines. They previously were speakers on their own national daily radio program, "Mid-Life Dimensions," broadcast on more than two hundred stations.

Jim served as a pastor for almost thirty years, while Sally served as pastor's wife. Sally also has been an elementary school remedial reading specialist. For five years Jim directed the Doctor of Ministry program at Talbot School of Theology, Biola University, and was associate professor of practical theology. Sally taught part-time at Talbot for five years.

Sally holds a Bachelor of Science degree in human development. Jim holds two earned master's degrees—one in psychology and one in theology—and two earned doctorates—a D.Min. in ministry and a Ph.D. in adult development and learning.

Jim and Sally have three daughters, three sons-in-law, three grandsons and four granddaughters.

To contact Jim and Sally Conway about speaking, write them c/o InterVarsity Press, P.O. Box 1400, Downers Grove, IL 60515.